MW01165086

FREE Test Taking Tips DVD Offer

To help us better serve you, we have developed a Test Taking Tips DVD that we would like to give you for FREE. **This DVD covers world-class test taking tips that you can use to be even more successful when you are taking your test.**

All that we ask is that you email us your feedback about your study guide. Please let us know what you thought about it – whether that is good, bad or indifferent.

To get your **FREE Test Taking Tips DVD**, email freedvd@studyguideteam.com with "FREE DVD" in the subject line and the following information in the body of the email:

    a. The title of your study guide.

    b. Your product rating on a scale of 1-5, with 5 being the highest rating.

    c. Your feedback about the study guide. What did you think of it?

    d. Your full name and shipping address to send your free DVD.

If you have any questions or concerns, please don't hesitate to contact us at freedvd@studyguideteam.com.

Thanks again!

SHSAT Prep Books 2018 & 2019

SHSAT Test Prep & SHSAT Practice Test Questions for the New York City SHSAT Exam

SHSAT Prep Books 2018-2019 Team

Table of Contents

Quick Overview

As you draw closer to taking your exam, effective preparation becomes more and more important. Thankfully, you have this study guide to help you get ready. Use this guide to help keep your studying on track and refer to it often.

This study guide contains several key sections that will help you be successful on your exam. The guide contains tips for what you should do the night before and the day of the test. Also included are test-taking tips. Knowing the right information is not always enough. Many well-prepared test takers struggle with exams. These tips will help equip you to accurately read, assess, and answer test questions.

A large part of the guide is devoted to showing you what content to expect on the exam and to helping you better understand that content. Near the end of this guide is a practice test so that you can see how well you have grasped the content. Then, answer explanations are provided so that you can understand why you missed certain questions.

Don't try to cram the night before you take your exam. This is not a wise strategy for a few reasons. First, your retention of the information will be low. Your time would be better used by reviewing information you already know rather than trying to learn a lot of new information. Second, you will likely become stressed as you try to gain a large amount of knowledge in a short amount of time. Third, you will be depriving yourself of sleep. So be sure to go to bed at a reasonable time the night before. Being well-rested helps you focus and remain calm.

Be sure to eat a substantial breakfast the morning of the exam. If you are taking the exam in the afternoon, be sure to have a good lunch as well. Being hungry is distracting and can make it difficult to focus. You have hopefully spent lots of time preparing for the exam. Don't let an empty stomach get in the way of success!

When travelling to the testing center, leave earlier than needed. That way, you have a buffer in case you experience any delays. This will help you remain calm and will keep you from missing your appointment time at the testing center.

Be sure to pace yourself during the exam. Don't try to rush through the exam. There is no need to risk performing poorly on the exam just so you can leave the testing center early. Allow yourself to use all of the allotted time if needed.

Remain positive while taking the exam even if you feel like you are performing poorly. Thinking about the content you should have mastered will not help you perform better on the exam.

Once the exam is complete, take some time to relax. Even if you feel that you need to take the exam again, you will be well served by some down time before you begin studying again. It's often easier to convince yourself to study if you know that it will come with a reward!

Test-Taking Strategies

1. Predicting the Answer

When you feel confident in your preparation for a multiple-choice test, try predicting the answer before reading the answer choices. This is especially useful on questions that test objective factual knowledge or that ask you to fill in a blank. By predicting the answer before reading the available choices, you eliminate the possibility that you will be distracted or led astray by an incorrect answer choice. You will feel more confident in your selection if you read the question, predict the answer, and then find your prediction among the answer choices. After using this strategy, be sure to still read all of the answer choices carefully and completely. If you feel unprepared, you should not attempt to predict the answers. This would be a waste of time and an opportunity for your mind to wander in the wrong direction.

2. Reading the Whole Question

Too often, test takers scan a multiple-choice question, recognize a few familiar words, and immediately jump to the answer choices. Test authors are aware of this common impatience, and they will sometimes prey upon it. For instance, a test author might subtly turn the question into a negative, or he or she might redirect the focus of the question right at the end. The only way to avoid falling into these traps is to read the entirety of the question carefully before reading the answer choices.

3. Looking for Wrong Answers

Long and complicated multiple-choice questions can be intimidating. One way to simplify a difficult multiple-choice question is to eliminate all of the answer choices that are clearly wrong. In most sets of answers, there will be at least one selection that can be dismissed right away. If the test is administered on paper, the test taker could draw a line through it to indicate that it may be ignored; otherwise, the test taker will have to perform this operation mentally or on scratch paper. In either case, once the obviously incorrect answers have been eliminated, the remaining choices may be considered. Sometimes identifying the clearly wrong answers will give the test taker some information about the correct answer. For instance, if one of the remaining answer choices is a direct opposite of one of the eliminated answer choices, it may well be the correct answer. The opposite of obviously wrong is obviously right! Of course, this is not always the case. Some answers are obviously incorrect simply because they are irrelevant to the question being asked. Still, identifying and eliminating some incorrect answer choices is a good way to simplify a multiple-choice question.

4. Don't Overanalyze

Anxious test takers often overanalyze questions. When you are nervous, your brain will often run wild, causing you to make associations and discover clues that don't actually exist. If you feel that this may be a problem for you, do whatever you can to slow down during the test. Try taking a deep breath or counting to ten. As you read and consider the question, restrict yourself to the particular words used by the author. Avoid thought tangents about what the author *really* meant, or what he or she was *trying* to say. The only things that matter on a multiple-choice test are the words that are actually in the question. You must avoid reading too much into a multiple-choice question, or supposing that the writer meant something other than what he or she wrote.

5. No Need for Panic

It is wise to learn as many strategies as possible before taking a multiple-choice test, but it is likely that you will come across a few questions for which you simply don't know the answer. In this situation, avoid panicking. Because most multiple-choice tests include dozens of questions, the relative value of a single wrong answer is small. Moreover, your failure on one question has no effect on your success elsewhere on the test. As much as possible, you should compartmentalize each question on a multiple-choice test. In other words, you should not allow your feelings about one question to affect your success on the others. When you find a question that you either don't understand or don't know how to answer, just take a deep breath and do your best. Read the entire question slowly and carefully. Try rephrasing the question a couple of different ways. Then, read all of the answer choices carefully. After eliminating obviously wrong answers, make a selection and move on to the next question.

6. Confusing Answer Choices

When working on a difficult multiple-choice question, there may be a tendency to focus on the answer choices that are the easiest to understand. Many people, whether consciously or not, gravitate to the answer choices that require the least concentration, knowledge, and memory. This is a mistake. When you come across an answer choice that is confusing, you should give it extra attention. A question might be confusing because you do not know the subject matter to which it refers. If this is the case, don't eliminate the answer before you have affirmatively settled on another. When you come across an answer choice of this type, set it aside as you look at the remaining choices. If you can confidently assert that one of the other choices is correct, you can leave the confusing answer aside. Otherwise, you will need to take a moment to try to better understand the confusing answer choice. Rephrasing is one way to tease out the sense of a confusing answer choice.

7. Your First Instinct

Many people struggle with multiple-choice tests because they overthink the questions. If you have studied sufficiently for the test, you should be prepared to trust your first instinct once you have carefully and completely read the question and all of the answer choices. There is a great deal of research suggesting that the mind can come to the correct conclusion very quickly once it has obtained all of the relevant information. At times, it may seem to you as if your intuition is working faster even than your reasoning mind. This may in fact be true. The knowledge you obtain while studying may be retrieved from your subconscious before you have a chance to work out the associations that support it. Verify your instinct by working out the reasons that it should be trusted.

8. Key Words

Many test takers struggle with multiple-choice questions because they have poor reading comprehension skills. Quickly reading and understanding a multiple-choice question requires a mixture of skill and experience. To help with this, try jotting down a few key words and phrases on a piece of scrap paper. Doing this concentrates the process of reading and forces the mind to weigh the relative importance of the question's parts. In selecting words and phrases to write down, the test taker thinks about the question more deeply and carefully. This is especially true for multiple-choice questions that are preceded by a long prompt.

9. Subtle Negatives

One of the oldest tricks in the multiple-choice test writer's book is to subtly reverse the meaning of a question with a word like *not* or *except*. If you are not paying attention to each word in the question, you can easily be led astray by this trick. For instance, a common question format is, "Which of the following is…?" Obviously, if the question instead is, "Which of the following is not…?," then the answer will be quite different. Even worse, the test makers are aware of the potential for this mistake and will include one answer choice that would be correct if the question were not negated or reversed. A test taker who misses the reversal will find what he or she believes to be a correct answer and will be so confident that he or she will fail to reread the question and discover the original error. The only way to avoid this is to practice a wide variety of multiple-choice questions and to pay close attention to each and every word.

10. Reading Every Answer Choice

It may seem obvious, but you should always read every one of the answer choices! Too many test takers fall into the habit of scanning the question and assuming that they understand the question because they recognize a few key words. From there, they pick the first answer choice that answers the question they believe they have read. Test takers who read all of the answer choices might discover that one of the latter answer choices is actually *more* correct. Moreover, reading all of the answer choices can remind you of facts related to the question that can help you arrive at the correct answer. Sometimes, a misstatement or incorrect detail in one of the latter answer choices will trigger your memory of the subject and will enable you to find the right answer. Failing to read all of the answer choices is like not reading all of the items on a restaurant menu: you might miss out on the perfect choice.

11. Spot the Hedges

One of the keys to success on multiple-choice tests is paying close attention to every word. This is never more true than with words like *almost*, *most*, *some*, and *sometimes*. These words are called "hedges" because they indicate that a statement is not totally true or not true in every place and time. An absolute statement will contain no hedges, but in many subjects, like literature and history, the answers are not always straightforward or absolute. There are always exceptions to the rules in these subjects. For this reason, you should favor those multiple-choice questions that contain hedging language. The presence of qualifying words indicates that the author is taking special care with his or her words, which is certainly important when composing the right answer. After all, there are many ways to be wrong, but there is only one way to be right! For this reason, it is wise to avoid answers that are absolute when taking a multiple-choice test. An absolute answer is one that says things are either all one way or all another. They often include words like *every*, *always*, *best*, and *never*. If you are taking a multiple-choice test in a subject that doesn't lend itself to absolute answers, be on your guard if you see any of these words.

12. Long Answers

In many subject areas, the answers are not simple. As already mentioned, the right answer often requires hedges. Another common feature of the answers to a complex or subjective question are qualifying clauses, which are groups of words that subtly modify the meaning of the sentence. If the question or answer choice describes a rule to which there are exceptions or the subject matter is complicated, ambiguous, or confusing, the correct answer will require many words in order to be expressed clearly and accurately. In essence, you should not be deterred by answer choices that seem excessively long. Oftentimes, the author of the text will not be able to write the correct answer without offering some qualifications and modifications. Your job is to read the answer choices thoroughly and completely and to select the one that most accurately and precisely answers the question.

13. Restating to Understand

Sometimes, a question on a multiple-choice test is difficult not because of what it asks but because of how it is written. If this is the case, restate the question or answer choice in different words. This process serves a couple of important purposes. First, it forces you to concentrate on the core of the question. In order to rephrase the question accurately, you have to understand it well. Rephrasing the question will concentrate your mind on the key words and ideas. Second, it will present the information to your mind in a fresh way. This process may trigger your memory and render some useful scrap of information picked up while studying.

14. True Statements

Sometimes an answer choice will be true in itself, but it does not answer the question. This is one of the main reasons why it is essential to read the question carefully and completely before proceeding to the answer choices. Too often, test takers skip ahead to the answer choices and look for true statements. Having found one of these, they are content to select it without reference to the question above. Obviously, this provides an easy way for test makers to play tricks. The savvy test taker will always read the entire question before turning to the answer choices. Then, having settled on a correct answer choice, he or she will refer to the original question and ensure that the selected answer is relevant. The mistake of choosing a correct-but-irrelevant answer choice is especially common on questions related to specific pieces of objective knowledge, like historical or scientific facts. A prepared test taker will have a wealth of factual knowledge at his or her disposal, and should not be careless in its application.

15. No Patterns

One of the more dangerous ideas that circulates about multiple-choice tests is that the correct answers tend to fall into patterns. These erroneous ideas range from a belief that B and C are the most common right answers, to the idea that an unprepared test-taker should answer "A-B-A-C-A-D-A-B-A." It cannot be emphasized enough that pattern-seeking of this type is exactly the WRONG way to approach a multiple-choice test. To begin with, it is highly unlikely that the test maker will plot the correct answers according to some predetermined pattern. The questions are scrambled and delivered in a random order. Furthermore, even if the test maker was following a pattern in the assignation of correct answers, there is no reason why the test taker would know which pattern he or she was using. Any attempt to discern a pattern in the answer choices is a waste of time and a distraction from the real work of taking the test. A test taker would be much better served by extra preparation before the test than by reliance on a pattern in the answers.

FREE DVD OFFER

Don't forget that doing well on your exam includes both understanding the test content and understanding how to use what you know to do well on the test. We offer a completely FREE Test Taking Tips DVD that covers world class test taking tips that you can use to be even more successful when you are taking your test.

All that we ask is that you email us your feedback about your study guide. To get your **FREE Test Taking Tips DVD**, email freedvd@studyguideteam.com with "FREE DVD" in the subject line and the following information in the body of the email:

- The title of your study guide.
- Your product rating on a scale of 1-5, with 5 being the highest rating.
- Your feedback about the study guide. What did you think of it?
- Your full name and shipping address to send your free DVD.

Introduction to the SHSAT

Function of the Test

The SHSAT is a standardized test that is used as the sole factor for admission to eight of New York City's Specialized High Schools. Fiorello H. LaGuardia High School is the only Specialized High School in New York City that does not require students to take the SHSAT exam as part of the admissions process. Students who are in the eighth or ninth grades who wish to attend one of these eight Specialized High Schools and who live in the five boroughs of New York City (Brooklyn, Manhattan, Queens, Staten Island, and The Bronx) must sit for this exam.

Test Administration

Each year, the SHSAT test is only offered in the month of October for eighth grade students and in the month of November for ninth grade students. Students who are interested in registering to take the exam can do so by talking with their school's guidance counselor. After students are registered, they will receive a test ticket to sit for the exam. Students who are sitting for the SHSAT exam must also rank (in order of priority) the Specialized High Schools that they would like to attend on their test ticket.

Students are able to take the SHSAT test twice—once in the eighth grade and once in the ninth grade—if they are not accepted to the Specialized High School of their choice after taking the exam in the eighth grade.

Students will be provided with the necessary accommodations for taking the exam, as long as the accommodations are permitted for the test. If necessary, mathematics glossaries can be provided in nine languages to students on the day of the exam.

Test Format

Students are given 180 minutes to complete the SHSAT, which is comprised of 57 questions in each of its two sections: English language arts (ELA) and math, as outlined in the table below. All of the reading and writing questions in the ELA section are multiple-choice and split between two categories. The first category requires students to utilize their revising and editing skills, while the second category assesses reading comprehension by asking students to extract information from various reading passages in order to answer associated questions. In the math section, there are 52 multiple-choice questions that deal with word and computational problems, as well as five grid-in questions that are *not* multiple-choice. These questions require students to provide correct numerical solutions to computational problems. Finally, all multiple-questions on both sections of the test have four answer choices per question, and both sections of the test each have ten unscored experimental questions that are used for field testing purposes for future iterations of the exam.

Sections of the SHSAT Test			
Subject Areas	**Questions (Multiple-Choice)***	**Question breakdown**	**Time Limit**
English Language Arts (ELA) Reading & Writing	57	20 revising/editing	180 minutes
		6 reading comprehension passages (5-7 questions for each)	
		10 experimental (unscored)	
Math	57	52 word &computational problems	
		5 grid-in questions*	
		10 experimental (unscored)	
Total Questions:	114		

Students are required to provide correct numerical answers for these questions

Scoring

Individuals are not penalized for wrong answers or for questions that are left blank. After completing the test, each student is given a raw score that is based on the number of questions answered correctly. Those raw scores are then converted into three digit composite scores (an 800 being the highest possible score). Scores are made available to the schools in March following the fall in which the exam was taken. For example, if a student takes the exam in the fall of 2017, his or her score will be released to the schools in the March of 2018.

One the test results are in, all students who took the SHSAT exam are ranked in order by composite score from highest to lowest. Seats are then filled in each of the Specialized High Schools, in order, according to the students' first choices until all of the open seats for that academic year are filled. The number of available seats at each of the Specialized High Schools varies from year to year.

Recent/Future Developments

The SHSAT was revised for the fall of 2017. Students were previously only given 150 minutes to complete the exam, which was formerly comprised of 45 questions in the verbal section and 50 questions in its math section (all in multiple-choice format). The reading and writing questions of the verbal section were split between three categories: scrambled paragraphs, logical reasoning, and reading comprehension passages. The math section was made up of a combination of word and computational problems. Finally, all multiple-choice questions on both sections of the test had five answer choices per question, and there were no experimental questions on the previous version of the exam.

English Language Arts

Reading Comprehension

Main Ideas and Supporting Details

Topics and main ideas are critical parts of writing. The *topic* is the subject matter of the piece. An example of a topic would be *global warming*.

The main idea is what the writer wants to say about that topic. A writer may make the point that global warming is a growing problem that must be addressed in order to save the planet. Therefore, the topic is global warming, and the main idea is that it's *a serious problem needing to be addressed*. The topic can be expressed in a word or two, but the main idea should be a complete thought.

An author will likely identify the topic immediately within the title or the first sentence of a passage. The main idea is usually presented in the introduction. In a single passage, the main idea may be identified in the first or last sentence, but it will most likely be directly stated and easily recognized by the reader. Because it is not always stated immediately in a passage, it's important to carefully read the entire passage to identify the main idea.

The main idea should not be confused with the thesis statement. A *thesis statement* is a clear statement of the writer's specific stance and can often be found in the introduction of a non-fiction piece. The thesis is a specific sentence (or two) that offers the direction and focus of the discussion.

In order to illustrate the main idea, a writer will use *supporting details*, the details that provide evidence or examples to help make a point. Supporting details often appear in the form of quotations, paraphrasing, or analysis. Authors should connect details and analysis to the main point.

For example, in the example of global warming, where the author's main idea is to show the seriousness of this growing problem and the need for change, the use of supporting details in this piece would be critical in effectively making that point. Supporting details used here might include *statistics* on an increase in global temperatures and *studies* showing the impact of global warming on the planet. The author could also include *projections* for future climate change in order to illustrate potential lasting effects of global warming.

It's important to evaluate the author's supporting details to be sure that they are credible, provide evidence of the author's point, and directly support the main idea. Though shocking statistics grab readers' attention, their use could be ineffective information in the piece. Details like this are crucial to understanding the passage and evaluating how well the author presents his or her argument and evidence.

Also remember that when most authors write, they want to make a point or send a message. This point or message of a text is known as the theme. Authors may state themes explicitly, like in *Aesop's Fables*. More often, especially in modern literature, readers must infer the theme based on text details. Usually after carefully reading and analyzing an entire text, the theme emerges. Typically, the longer the piece, the more themes you will encounter, though often one theme dominates the rest, as evidenced by the author's purposeful revisiting of it throughout the passage.

Summarizing a Complex Text

A summary is a shortened version of the original text, written by the reader in their own words. In order to effectively summarize a more complex text, it is necessary to fully understand the original source, and to highlight the major points covered. It may be helpful to outline the original text to get a big picture view of it, and to avoid getting bogged down in the minor details. For example, a summary wouldn't need to include a specific statistic from the original source unless it was the major focus of the piece. Also, it's important for readers to use their own words, but to retain the original meaning of the passage. The key to a good summary is to emphasize the main idea without changing the focus of the original information.

Paraphrasing calls for the reader to take a small part of the passage and list or describe its main points. Paraphrasing is more than rewording the original passage, though. Like summary, it should be written in the reader's own words, while still retaining the meaning of the original source. The main difference between summarizing and paraphrasing is the length of the original passage. A summary would be appropriate for a much larger piece, while paraphrase might focus on just a few lines of text. Effective paraphrasing will indicate an understanding of the original source, yet still help the reader expand on their interpretation. A paraphrase should neither add new information nor remove essential facts that will change the meaning of the source.

Recognizing the Structure of Texts in Various Formats

Writing can be classified under four passage types: narrative, expository, descriptive (sometimes called technical), and persuasive. Though these types are not mutually exclusive, one form tends to dominate the rest. By recognizing the *type* of passage you're reading, you gain insight into *how* you should read. If you're reading a narrative, you can assume the author intends to entertain, which means you may skim the text without losing meaning. A technical document might require a close read, because skimming the passage might cause the reader to miss salient details.

1. *Narrative* writing, at its core, is the art of storytelling. For a narrative to exist, certain elements must be present. It must have characters. While many characters are human, characters could be defined as anything that thinks, acts, and talks like a human. For example, many recent movies, such as *Lord of the Rings* and *The Chronicles of Narnia*, include animals, fantastical creatures, and even trees that behave like humans. It must have a plot or sequence of events. Typically, those events follow a standard plot diagram, but recent trends start *in medias res* or in the middle (near the climax). In this instance, foreshadowing and flashbacks often fill in plot details. Along with characters and a plot, there must also be conflict. Conflict is usually divided into two types: internal and external. Internal conflict indicates the character is in turmoil. Internal conflicts are presented through the character's thoughts. External conflicts are visible. Types of external conflict include a person versus nature, another person, and society.

2. *Expository writing is detached and to the point.* Since expository writing is designed to instruct or inform, it usually involves directions and steps written in second person ("you" voice) and lacks any persuasive or narrative elements. Sequence words such as *first*, *second*, and *third*, or *in the first place*, *secondly*, and *lastly* are often given to add fluency and cohesion. Common examples of expository writing include instructor's lessons, cookbook recipes, and repair manuals.

3. Due to its empirical nature, *technical* writing is filled with steps, charts, graphs, data, and statistics. The goal of technical writing is to advance understanding in a field through the scientific method. Experts such as teachers, doctors, or mechanics use words unique to the profession in which they

operate. These words, which often incorporate acronyms, are called *jargon*. Technical writing is a type of expository writing, but is not meant to be understood by the general public. Instead, technical writers assume readers have received a formal education in a particular field of study, and need no explanation as to what the jargon means. Imagine a doctor trying to understand a diagnostic reading for a car or a mechanic trying to interpret lab results. Only professionals with proper training will fully comprehend the text.

4. *Persuasive* writing is designed to change opinions and attitudes. The topic, stance, and arguments are found in the thesis, positioned near the end of the introduction. Later supporting paragraphs offer relevant quotations, paraphrases, and summaries from primary or secondary sources, which are then interpreted, analyzed, and evaluated. The goal of persuasive writers is not to stack quotes, but to develop original ideas by using sources as a starting point. Good persuasive writing makes powerful arguments with valid sources and thoughtful analysis. Poor persuasive writing is riddled with bias and logical fallacies. Sometimes, logical and illogical arguments are sandwiched together in the same piece. Therefore, readers should display skepticism when reading persuasive arguments.

Understanding Literary Interpretation

Literary interpretation is an interpretation and analysis of a literary work, based on the textual evidence in the work. It is often subjective as critical readers may discern different meanings in the details. A test taker needs to be prepared for questions that will test how well he or she can read a passage, make an analysis, and then provide evidence to support that analysis.

Literal and Figurative Meanings
When analyzing and interpreting fiction, readers must be active participants in the experience. Some authors make their messages clearer than others, but the onus is on the reader to add layers to what is read through interpretation. In literary interpretation, the goal is not to offer an opinion as to the inherent value of the work. Rather, the goal is to determine what the text means by analyzing the *literal and figurative meanings* of the text through critical reading.

Critical reading is close reading that elicits questions as the reader progresses. Many authors of fiction use literary elements and devices to further theme and to speak to their audience. These elements often utilize language that has an alternate or figurative meaning in addition to their actual or literal meaning. Readers should be asking questions about these and other important details as a passage is analyzed. What unfamiliar words are there? What is their contextual definition? How do they contribute to the overall feel of the work? How do they contribute to the mood and general message? Literal and figurative meanings are discussed further in the informational texts and rhetoric section.

Drawing Inferences
An *inference* refers to a point that is implied (as opposed to directly-stated) by the evidence presented. It's necessary to use inference in order to draw conclusions about the meaning of a passage. Authors make implications through character dialogue, thoughts, effects on others, actions, and looks.

When making an inference about a passage, it's important to rely only on the information that is provided in the text itself. This helps readers ensure that their conclusions are valid. Drawing inferences is also discussed in the informational texts and rhetoric section.

Textual Evidence
It's helpful to read a passage a few times, noting details that seem important to the piece. Textual evidence within the details helps readers draw a conclusion about a passage. *Textual evidence* refers to

information—facts and examples that support the main idea. Textual evidence will likely come from outside sources and can be in the form of quoted or paraphrased material. In order to draw a conclusion from evidence, it's important to examine the credibility and validity of that evidence as well as how (and if) it relates to the main idea. Effective use of textual evidence should connect to the main idea and support a specific point. Textual evidence is examined further in the informational texts and rhetoric section.

Understanding the Development of Themes

Identifying Theme or Central Message
The *theme* is the central message of a fictional work, whether that work is structured as prose, drama, or poetry. It is the heart of what an author is trying to say to readers through the writing, and theme is largely conveyed through literary elements and techniques.

In literature, a theme can often be determined by considering the over-arching narrative conflict within the work. Though there are several types of conflicts and several potential themes within them, the following are the most common:

- *Individual against the self*—relevant to themes of self-awareness, internal struggles, pride, coming of age, facing reality, fate, free will, vanity, loss of innocence, loneliness, isolation, fulfillment, failure, and disillusionment

- *Individual against nature*— relevant to themes of knowledge vs. ignorance, nature as beauty, quest for discovery, self-preservation, chaos and order, circle of life, death, and destruction of beauty

- *Individual against society*— relevant to themes of power, beauty, good, evil, war, class struggle, totalitarianism, role of men/women, wealth, corruption, change vs. tradition, capitalism, destruction, heroism, injustice, and racism

- *Individual against another individual*— relevant to themes of hope, loss of love or hope, sacrifice, power, revenge, betrayal, and honor

For example, in Hawthorne's *The Scarlet Letter*, one possible narrative conflict could be the individual against the self, with a relevant theme of internal struggles. This theme is alluded to through characterization—Dimmesdale's moral struggle with his love for Hester and Hester's internal struggles with the truth and her daughter, Pearl. It's also alluded to through plot—Dimmesdale's suicide and Hester helping the very townspeople who initially condemned her.

Sometimes, a text can convey a *message* or *universal lesson*—a truth or insight that the reader infers from the text, based on analysis of the literary and/or poetic elements. This message is often presented as a statement. For example, a potential message in Shakespeare's *Hamlet* could be "Revenge is what ultimately drives the human soul." This message can be immediately determined through plot and characterization in numerous ways, but it can also be determined through the setting of Norway, which is bordering on war.

How Authors Develop Theme
Authors employ a variety of techniques to present a theme. They may compare or contrast characters, events, places, ideas, or historical or invented settings to speak thematically. They may use analogies, metaphors, similes, allusions, or other literary devices to convey the theme. An author's use of diction,

syntax, and tone can also help convey the theme. Authors will often develop themes through the development of characters, use of the setting, repetition of ideas, use of symbols, and through contrasting value systems. Authors of both fiction and nonfiction genres will use a variety of these techniques to develop one or more themes.

Regardless of the literary genre, there are commonalities in how authors, playwrights, and poets develop themes or central ideas.

Authors often do research, the results of which contributes to theme. In prose fiction and drama, this research may include real historical information about the setting the author has chosen or include elements that make fictional characters, settings, and plots seem realistic to the reader. In nonfiction, research is critical since the information contained within this literature must be accurate and, moreover, accurately represented.

In fiction, authors present a narrative conflict that will contribute to the overall theme. In fiction, this conflict may involve the storyline itself and some trouble within characters that needs resolution. In nonfiction, this conflict may be an explanation or commentary on factual people and events.

Authors will sometimes use character motivation to convey theme, such as in the example from *Hamlet* regarding revenge. In fiction, the characters an author creates will think, speak, and act in ways that effectively convey the theme to readers. In nonfiction, the characters are factual, as in a biography, but authors pay particular attention to presenting those motivations to make them clear to readers.

Authors also use literary devices as a means of conveying theme. For example, the use of moon symbolism in Shelley's *Frankenstein* is significant as its phases can be compared to the phases that the Creature undergoes as he struggles with his identity.

The selected point of view can also contribute to a work's theme. The use of first person point of view in a fiction or non-fiction work engages the reader's response differently than third person point of view. The central idea or theme from a first-person narrative may differ from a third-person limited text.

In literary nonfiction, authors usually identify the purpose of their writing, which differs from fiction, where the general purpose is to entertain. The purpose of nonfiction is usually to inform, persuade, or entertain the audience. The stated purpose of a non-fiction text will drive how the central message or theme, if applicable, is presented.

Authors identify an audience for their writing, which is critical in shaping the theme of the work. For example, the audience for J.K. Rowling's *Harry Potter* series would be different than the audience for a biography of George Washington. The audience an author chooses to address is closely tied to the purpose of the work. The choice of an audience also drives the choice of language and level of diction an author uses. Ultimately, the intended audience determines the level to which that subject matter is presented and the complexity of the theme.

Evaluating the Author's Point of View in a Given Text

When it comes to authors' writings, readers should always identify a position or stance. No matter how objective a piece may seem, assume the author has preconceived beliefs. Reduce the likelihood of accepting an invalid argument by looking for multiple articles on the topic, including those with varying opinions. If several opinions point in the same direction, and are backed by reputable peer-reviewed sources, it's more likely the author has a valid argument. Positions that run contrary to widely held beliefs and existing data should invite scrutiny. There are exceptions to the rule, so be a careful consumer of information.

Though themes, symbols, and motifs are buried deep within the text and can sometimes be difficult to infer, an author's purpose is usually obvious from the beginning. There are four purposes of writing: to inform, to persuade, to describe, and to entertain. Informative writings present facts in an accessible way. Persuasive writing is appeals to emotions and logic to inspire the reader to adopt a specific stance. Be wary of this type of writing, as it often lacks objectivity. Descriptive writing is designed to paint a picture in the reader's mind, while writings that entertain are often narratives designed to engage and delight the reader.

The various writing styles are usually blended, with one purpose dominating the rest. For example, a persuasive piece might begin with a humorous tale to make readers more receptive to the persuasive message, or a recipe in a cookbook designed to inform might be preceded by an entertaining anecdote that makes the recipe more appealing.

Identifying Literary Elements

There is no one, final definition of what literary elements are. They can be considered features or characteristics of fiction, but they are really more of a way that readers can unpack a text for the purpose of analysis and understanding the meaning. The elements contribute to a reader's literary interpretation of a passage as to how they function to convey the central message of a work. The most common literary elements used for analysis are the presented below.

Point of View
The *point of view* is the position the narrator takes when telling the story in prose. If a narrator is incorporated in a drama, the point of view may vary; in poetry, point of view refers to the position the speaker in a poem takes.

First Person
The first person point of view is when the writer uses the word "I" in the text. Poetry often uses first person, e.g., William Wordsworth's "I Wandered Lonely as a Cloud." Two examples of prose written in first person are Suzanne Collins' *The Hunger Games* and Anthony Burgess's *A Clockwork Orange*.

Second Person
The second person point of view is when the writer uses the pronoun "you." It is not widely used in prose fiction, but as a technique, it has been used by writers such as William Faulkner in *Absalom, Absalom!* and Albert Camus in *The Fall*. It is more common in poetry—e.g., Pablo Neruda's "If You Forget Me."

Third Person
Third person point of view is when the writer utilizes pronouns such as him, her, or them. It may be the most utilized point of view in prose as it provides flexibility to an author and is the one with which readers are most familiar. There are two main types of third person used in fiction. *Third person omniscient* uses a narrator that is all-knowing, relating the story by conveying and interpreting thoughts/feelings of all characters. In *third person limited,* the narrator relates the story through the perspective of one character's thoughts/feelings, usually the main character.

Plot

The *plot* is what happens in the story. Plots may be singular, containing one problem, or they may be very complex, with many sub-plots. All plots have exposition, a conflict, a climax, and a resolution. The *conflict* drives the plot and is something that the reader expects to be resolved. The plot carries those events along until there is a resolution to the conflict.

Tone

The *tone* of a story reflects the author's attitude and opinion about the subject matter of the story or text. Tone can be expressed through word choice, imagery, figurative language, syntax, and other details. The emotion or mood the reader experiences relates back to the tone of the story. Some examples of possible tones are humorous, somber, sentimental, and ironic.

Setting

The *setting* is the time, place, or set of surroundings in which the story occurs. It includes time or time span, place(s), climates, geography—man-made or natural—or cultural environments. Emily Dickinson's poem "Because I could not stop for Death" has a simple setting—the narrator's symbolic ride with Death through town towards the local graveyard. Conversely, Leo Tolstoy's *War and Peace* encompasses numerous settings within settings in the areas affected by the Napoleonic Wars, spanning 1805 to 1812.

Characters

Characters are the story's figures that assume primary, secondary, or minor roles. *Central* or *major* characters are those integral to the story—the plot cannot be resolved without them. A central character can be a *protagonist* or hero. There may be more than one protagonist, and he/she doesn't always have to possess good characteristics. A character can also be an *antagonist*—the force against a protagonist.

Dynamic characters change over the course of the plot time. *Static* characters do not change. A *symbolic* character is one that represents an author's idea about society in general—e.g., Napoleon in Orwell's *Animal Farm*. *Stock* characters are those that appear across genres and embrace stereotypes—e.g., the cowboy of the Wild West or the blonde bombshell in a detective novel. A *flat* character is one that does not present a lot of complexity or depth, while a *rounded* character does. Sometimes, the *narrator* of a story or the *speaker* in a poem can be a character—e.g., Nick Carraway in F. Scott Fitzgerald's *The Great Gatsby* or the speaker in Robert Browning's "My Last Duchess." The narrator might also function as a character in prose, though not be part of the story—e.g., Charles Dickens' narrator of *A Christmas Carol*.

Understanding Figurative Language

Whereas literal language is the author's use of precise words, proper meanings, definitions, and phrases that mean exactly what they say, *figurative language* deviates from precise meaning and word definition—often in conjunction with other familiar words and phrases—to paint a picture for the reader. Figurative language is less explicit and more open to reader interpretation.

Some examples of figurative language are included in the following graphic.

	Definition	Example
Simile	Compares two things using "like" or "as"	Her hair was like gold.
Metaphor	Compares two things as if they are the same	He was a giant teddy bear.
Idiom	Using words with predictable meanings to create a phrase with a different meaning	The world is your oyster.
Alliteration	Repeating the same beginning sound or letter in a phrase for emphasis	The busy baby babbled.
Personification	Attributing human characteristics to an object or an animal	The house glowered menacingly with a dark smile.
Foreshadowing	Giving an indication that something is going to happen later in the story	I wasn't aware at the time, but I would come to regret those words.
Symbolism	Using symbols to represent ideas and provide a different meaning	The ring represented the bond between us.
Onomatopoeia	Using words that imitate sound	The tire went off with a bang and a crunch.
Imagery	Appealing to the senses by using descriptive language	The sky was painted with red and pink and streaked with orange.
Hyperbole	Using exaggeration not meant to be taken literally	The girl weighed less than a feather.

Figurative language can be used to give additional insight into the theme or message of a text by moving beyond the usual and literal meaning of words and phrases. It can also be used to appeal to the senses of readers and create a more in-depth story.

Understanding Poetic Devices and Structure

Poetic Devices
Rhyme is the poet's use of corresponding word sounds in order to create an effect. Most rhyme occurs at the ends of a poem's lines, which is how readers arrive at the *rhyme scheme*. Each line that has a corresponding rhyming sound is assigned a letter—A, B, C, and so on. When using a rhyme scheme, poets will often follow lettered patterns. Robert Frost's *"The Road Not Taken"* uses the ABAAB rhyme scheme:

Two roads diverged in a yellow wood,	A
And sorry I could not travel both	B
And be one traveler, long I stood	A
And looked down one as far as I could	A
To where it bent in the undergrowth;	B

Another important poetic device is *rhythm*—metered patterns within poetry verses. When a poet develops rhythm through *meter*, he or she is using a combination of stressed and unstressed syllables to create a sound effect for the reader.

Rhythm is created by the use of *poetic feet*—individual rhythmic units made up of the combination of stressed and unstressed syllables. A line of poetry is made up of one or more poetic feet. There are five standard types in English poetry, as depicted in the chart below.

Foot Type	Rhythm	Pattern
Iamb	buh Buh	Unstressed/stressed
Trochee	Buh buh	Stressed/unstressed
Spondee	Buh Buh	Stressed/stressed
Anapest	buh buh Buh	Unstressed/unstressed/stressed
Dactyl	Buh buh buh	Stressed/unstressed/unstressed

Structure

Poetry is most easily recognized by its structure, which varies greatly. For example, a structure may be strict in the number of lines it uses. It may use rhyming patterns or may not rhyme at all. There are three main types of poetic structures:

- *Verse*—poetry with a consistent meter and rhyme scheme
- *Blank verse*—poetry with consistent meter but an inconsistent rhyme scheme
- *Free verse*—poetry with inconsistent meter or rhyme

Verse poetry is most often developed in the form of *stanzas*—groups of word lines. Stanzas can also be considered *verses*. The structure is usually formulaic and adheres to the protocols for the form. For example, the English *sonnet* form uses a structure of fourteen lines and a variety of different rhyming patterns. The English *ode* typically uses three ten-line stanzas and has a particular rhyming pattern.

Poets choose poetic structure based on the effect they want to create. Some structures—such as the ballad and haiku—developed out of cultural influences and common artistic practice in history, but in more modern poetry, authors choose their structure to best fit their intended effect.

Literary Structure: Prose and Poetry

Structure refers to how a writer organizes ideas. In literature, a text may be either *prose* or *poetry*. Poetry relies on careful word choice (especially in terms of sound and emotional meaning) and rhythm in order to communicate a special feeling or idea. Contrary to the popular assumption, poetry doesn't have to rhyme or follow a strict structure. In fact, there are two types of poetic form: *open form* and *closed form*. In closed form, the poet follows a predictable and repetitive structure, perhaps by using a fixed number of syllables in each line or repeating the same rhyme scheme. Examples of closed-form structure include sonnets and haiku, both of which require the poet to follow an established pattern of rhythm or rhyme. Open-form poetry doesn't have restrictions on length, the number of syllables or pattern of stress in each line (also known as meter), or the rhyme pattern. Open-form poetry has a structure, but it's more flexible and open to the creative whims of the poet. When a poet uses open form, changes in structure can reflect changes in emotion. For example, if a poem starts out with blunt, brief lines but then develops into long and complex lines, it might represent the speaker becoming more open and expressive of emotions that they had previously been reluctant to share.

Prose is regular written language without any meter or rhythmic form. Literary prose includes novels, short stories, and memoirs. An author may choose prose over poetry when they want to communicate in colloquial language, or when they want to convey information that is more straightforward (but of course, both poetry and prose can be emotional and creative). It's also possible to combine prose and poetry. In Shakespeare's plays, for example, some characters speak in metered lines while other characters speak in prose. This separation may indicate the topic under discussion. For example, in *Julius Caesar*, Brutus' speech is in prose, while Marc Antony's speech is written in iambic pentameter, a common poetic meter. Antony's speech begins with "Friends, Romans, countrymen, lend me your ears; / I come to bury Caesar, not to praise him." The cadence and stress of the language in Antony's speech makes for a more powerful listening device compared to Brutus' opening, "Romans, countrymen, and friends! Listen to my reasons and be silent so you can hear." In this way, employing prose or poetry can influence the impression that readers get from a text or drama. The crowd, in *Julius Caesar*, is persuaded by Marc Antony's speech in the end, for all its rhetorical glory.

Understanding the Effect of Word Choice

An author's choice of words—also referred to as *diction*—helps to convey his or her meaning in a particular way. Through diction, an author can convey a particular tone—e.g., a humorous tone, a serious tone—in order to support the thesis in a meaningful way to the reader.

Connotation and Denotation
Connotation is when an author chooses words or phrases that invoke ideas or feelings other than their literal meaning. An example of the use of connotation is the word *cheap*, which suggests something is poor in value or negatively describes a person as reluctant to spend money. When something or someone is described this way, the reader is more inclined to have a particular image or feeling about it or him/her. Thus, connotation can be a very effective language tool in creating emotion and swaying opinion. However, connotations are sometimes hard to pin down because varying emotions can be associated with a word. Generally, though, connotative meanings tend to be fairly consistent within a specific cultural group.

Denotation refers to words or phrases that mean exactly what they say. It is helpful when a writer wants to present hard facts or vocabulary terms with which readers may be unfamiliar. Some examples of denotation are the words *inexpensive* and *frugal*. *Inexpensive* refers to the cost of something, not its value, and *frugal* indicates that a person is conscientiously watching his or her spending. These terms do not elicit the same emotions that *cheap* does.

Authors sometimes choose to use both, but what they choose and when they use it is what critical readers need to differentiate. One method isn't inherently better than the other; however, one may create a better effect, depending upon an author's intent. If, for example, an author's purpose is to inform, to instruct, and to familiarize readers with a difficult subject, his or her use of connotation may be helpful. However, it may also undermine credibility and confuse readers. An author who wants to create a credible, scholarly effect in his or her text would most likely use denotation, which emphasizes literal, factual meaning and examples.

Technical Language
Test takers and critical readers alike should be very aware of technical language used within informational text. *Technical language* refers to terminology that is specific to a particular industry and is best understood by those specializing in that industry. This language is fairly easy to differentiate, since it will most likely be unfamiliar to readers. It's critical to be able to define technical language either

by the author's written definition, through the use of an included glossary—if offered—or through context clues that help readers clarify word meaning.

Identifying Rhetorical Strategies

Rhetoric refers to an author's use of particular strategies, appeals, and devices to persuade an intended audience. The more effective the use of rhetoric, the more likely the audience will be persuaded.

Determining an Author's Point of View

A *rhetorical strategy*—also referred to as a *rhetorical mode*—is the structural way an author chooses to present his/her argument. Though the terms noted below are similar to the organizational structures noted earlier, these strategies do not imply that the entire text follows the approach. For example, a cause and effect organizational structure is solely that, nothing more. A persuasive text may use cause and effect as a strategy to convey a singular point. Thus, an argument may include several of the strategies as the author strives to convince his or her audience to take action or accept a different point of view. It's important that readers are able to identify an author's thesis and position on the topic in order to be able to identify the careful construction through which the author speaks to the reader. The following are some of the more common rhetorical strategies:

- *Cause and effect*—establishing a logical correlation or causation between two ideas
- *Classification/division*—the grouping of similar items together or division of something into parts
- *Comparison/contrast*—the distinguishing of similarities/differences to expand on an idea
- *Definition*—used to clarify abstract ideas, unfamiliar concepts, or to distinguish one idea from another
- *Description*—use of vivid imagery, active verbs, and clear adjectives to explain ideas
- *Exemplification*—the use of examples to explain an idea
- *Narration*—anecdotes or personal experience to present or expand on a concept
- *Problem/Solution*—presentation of a problem or problems, followed by proposed solution(s)

Rhetorical Strategies and Devices

A *rhetorical device* is the phrasing and presentation of an idea that reinforces and emphasizes a point in an argument. A rhetorical device is often quite memorable. One of the more famous uses of a rhetorical device is in John F. Kennedy's 1961 inaugural address: "Ask not what your country can do for you, ask what you can do for your country." The contrast of ideas presented in the phrasing is an example of the rhetorical device of antimetabole. Some other common examples are provided below, but test takers should be aware that this is not a complete list.

Device	Definition	Example
Allusion	A reference to a famous person, event, or significant literary text as a form of significant comparison	"We are apt to shut our eyes against a painful truth, and listen to the song of that siren till she transforms us into beasts." Patrick Henry
Anaphora	The repetition of the same words at the beginning of successive words, phrases, or clauses, designed to emphasize an idea	"We shall not flag or fail. We shall go on to the end. We shall fight in France, we shall fight on the seas and oceans, we shall fight with growing confidence … we shall fight in the fields and in the streets, we shall fight in the hills. We shall never surrender." Winston Churchill
Understatement	A statement meant to portray a situation as less important than it actually is to create an ironic effect	"The war in the Pacific has not necessarily developed in Japan's favor." Emperor Hirohito, surrendering Japan in World War II
Parallelism	A syntactical similarity in a structure or series of structures used for impact of an idea, making it memorable	"A penny saved is a penny earned." Ben Franklin
Rhetorical question	A question posed that is not answered by the writer though there is a desired response, most often designed to emphasize a point	"Can anyone look at our reduced standing in the world today and say, 'Let's have four more years of this?'" Ronald Reagan

Literature refers to a collection of written works that are the distinctive voices of peoples, time periods, and cultures. The world has gained great insight into human thought, vices, virtues, and desires through the written word. As the work pertains to the author's approach to these insights, literature can be classified as fiction or non-fiction.

Understanding the Characteristics of Literary Genres

Classifying literature involves an understanding of the concept of genre. A *genre* is a category of literature that possesses similarities in style and in characteristics. Based on form and structure, there are four basic genres.

Fictional Prose
Fictional prose consists of fictional works written in standard form with a natural flow of speech and without poetic structure. Fictional prose primarily utilizes grammatically complete sentences and a paragraph structure to convey its message.

Drama
Drama is fiction that is written to be performed in a variety of media, intended to be performed for an audience, and structured for that purpose. It might be composed using poetry or prose, often straddling the elements of both in what actors are expected to present. Action and dialogue are the tools used in drama to tell the story.

Poetry
Poetry is fiction in verse that has a unique focus on the rhythm of language and focuses on intensity of feeling. It is not an entire story, though it may tell one; it is compact in form and in function. Poetry can be considered as a poet's brief word picture for a reader. Poetic structure is primarily composed of lines and stanzas. Together, poetic structure and devices are the methods that poets use to lead readers to feeling an effect and, ultimately, to the interpretive message.

Literary Nonfiction
Literary nonfiction is prose writing that is based on current or past real events or real people and includes straightforward accounts as well as those that offer opinions on facts or factual events. The GED exam distinguishes between *literary nonfiction*—a form of writing that incorporates literary styles and techniques to create factually-based narratives—and informational texts, which will be addressed in the next section.

Identifying Characteristics of Major Forms Within Each Genre

Fictional Prose
Fiction written in prose can be further broken down into *fiction genres*—types of fiction. Some of the more common genres of fiction are as follows:

- *Classical Fiction*—a work of fiction considered timeless in its message or theme, remaining noteworthy and meaningful over decades or centuries—e.g., Charlotte **Brontë's** *Jane Eyre*, Mark Twain's *Adventures of Huckleberry Finn*

- *Fables*— short fiction that generally features animals, fantastic creatures, or other forces within nature that assume human-like characters and has a moral lesson for the reader—e.g., Aesop's Fables

- *Fairy tales*—children's stories with magical characters in imaginary, enchanted lands, usually depicting a struggle between good and evil, a sub-genre of folklore—e.g., Hans Christian Anderson's *The Little Mermaid*, *Cinderella* by the Brothers Grimm

- *Fantasy*—fiction with magic or supernatural elements that cannot occur in the real world, sometimes involving medieval elements in language, usually includes some form of sorcery or witchcraft and sometimes set on a different world—e.g., J.R.R. Tolkien's *The Hobbit*, J.K. Rowling's *Harry Potter and the Sorcerer's Stone*, George R.R. Martin's *A Game of Thrones*

- *Folklore*—types of fiction passed down from oral tradition, stories indigenous to a particular region or culture, with a local flavor in tone, designed to help humans cope with their condition in life and validate cultural traditions, beliefs, and customs—e.g., William Laughead's *Paul Bunyan and The Blue Ox*, the Buddhist story of "The Banyan Deer"

- *Mythology*—closely related to folklore but more widespread, features mystical, otherworldly characters and addresses the basic question of why and how humans exist, relies heavily on allegory and features gods or heroes captured in some sort of struggle—e.g., Greek myths, Genesis I and II in the *Bible*, Arthurian legends

- *Science fiction*—fiction that uses the principle of *extrapolation*—loosely defined as a form of prediction—to imagine future realities and problems of the human experience—e.g., Robert Heinlein's *Stranger in a Strange Land*, Ayn Rand's *Anthem*, Isaac Asimov's *I, Robot*, Philip K. Dick's *Do Androids Dream of Electric Sheep*?

- *Short stories*—short works of prose fiction with fully-developed themes and characters, focused on mood, generally developed with a single plot, with a short period of time for settings—e.g., Edgar Allan Poe's "Fall of the House of Usher," Shirley Jackson's "The Lottery," Isaac Bashevis Singer's "Gimpel the Fool"

Drama

Drama refers to a form of literature written for the purpose of performance for an audience. Like prose fiction, drama has several genres. The following are the most common ones:

- *Comedy*—a humorous play designed to amuse and entertain, often with an emphasis on the common person's experience, generally resolved in a positive way—e.g., Richard Sheridan's *School for Scandal*, Shakespeare's *Taming of the Shrew*, Neil Simon's *The Odd Couple*

- *History*—a play based on recorded history where the fate of a nation or kingdom is at the core of the conflict—e.g., Christopher Marlowe's *Edward II*, Shakespeare's *King Richard III*, Arthur Miller's *The Crucible*

- *Tragedy*—a serious play that often involves the downfall of the protagonist, in modern tragedies, the protagonist is not necessarily in a position of power or authority—e.g., Jean Racine's *Phèdre*, Arthur Miller's *Death of a Salesman*, John Steinbeck's *Of Mice and Men*

- *Melodrama*—a play that is emphasizes heightened emotion and sensationalism, generally with stereotypical characters in exaggerated or realistic situations and with moral polarization—e.g., Jean-Jacques Rousseau's *Pygmalion*

- *Tragi-comedy*—a play that has elements of both tragedy—a character experiencing a tragic loss—and comedy—the resolution is often positive with no clear distinctive mood for either—e.g., Shakespeare's *The Merchant of Venice*, Anton Chekhov's *The Cherry Orchard*

Poetry

The genre of *poetry* refers to literary works that focus on the expression of feelings and ideas through the use of structure and linguistic rhythm to create a desired effect.

Different poetic structures and devices are used to create the various major forms of poetry. Some of the most common forms are discussed in the following chart.

Type	Poetic Structure	Example
Ballad	A poem or song passed down orally which tells a story and in English tradition usually uses an ABAB or ABCB rhyme scheme	William Butler Yeats' "The Ballad Of Father O'Hart"
Epic	A long poem from ancient oral tradition which narrates the story of a legendary or heroic protagonist	Homer's The Odyssey Virgil's The Aeneid
Haiku	A Japanese poem of three unrhymed lines with five, seven, and five syllables (in English) with nature as a common subject matter	Matsuo Bashō An old silent pond... A frog jumps into the pond, splash! Silence again.
Limerick	A five-line poem written in an AABBA rhyme scheme, with a witty focus	From Edward Lear's Book of Nonsense— "There was a Young Person of Smyrna Whose grandmother threatened to burn her..."
Ode	A formal lyric poem that addresses and praises a person, place, thing, or idea	Edna St. Vincent Millay's "Ode To Silence"
Sonnet	A fourteen-line poem written in iambic pentameter	Shakespeare's Sonnets 18 and 130

Nonfiction works are best characterized by their subject matter, which must be factual and real, describing true life experiences. There are several common types of literary non-fiction.

Biography

A *biography* is a work written about a real person (historical or currently living). It involves factual accounts of the person's life, often in a re-telling of those events based on available, researched factual information. The re-telling and dialogue, especially if related within quotes, must be accurate and reflect reliable sources. A biography reflects the time and place in which the person lived, with the goal of creating an understanding of the person and his/her human experience. Examples of well-known biographies include *The Life of Samuel Johnson* by James Boswell and *Steve Jobs* by Walter Isaacson.

Autobiography

An *autobiography* is a factual account of a person's life written by that person. It may contain some or all of the same elements as a biography, but the author is the subject matter. An autobiography will be told in first person narrative. Examples of well-known autobiographies in literature include *Night* by Elie Wiesel and *Margaret Thatcher: The Autobiography* by Margaret Thatcher.

Memoir

A *memoir* is a historical account of a person's life and experiences written by one who has personal, intimate knowledge of the information. The line between memoir, autobiography, and biography is often muddled, but generally speaking, a memoir covers a specific timeline of events as opposed to the other forms of nonfiction. A memoir is less all-encompassing. It is also less formal in tone and tends to focus on the emotional aspect of the presented timeline of events. Some examples of memoirs in literature include *Angela's Ashes* by Frank McCourt and *All Creatures Great and Small* by James Herriot.

Journalism

Some forms of *journalism* can fall into the category of literary non-fiction—e.g., travel writing, nature writing, sports writing, the interview, and sometimes, the essay. Some examples include Elizabeth Kolbert's "The Lost World, in the Annals of Extinction series for *The New Yorker* and Gary Smith's "Ali and His Entourage" for ***Sports Illustrated***.

Informational Texts

Informational texts are a category of texts within the genre of nonfiction. Their intent is to inform, and while they do convey a point of view and may include literary devices, they do not utilize other literary elements, such as characters or plot. An informational text also reflects a *thesis*—an implicit or explicit statement of the text's intent and/or a *main idea*—the overarching focus and/or purpose of the text, generally implied. Some examples of informational texts are informative articles, instructional/how-to texts, factual reports, reference texts, and self-help texts.

Interpreting Textual Evidence in Informational Text
Literal and Figurative Meanings
It is important when evaluating informational texts to consider the use of both *literal and figurative meanings*. The words and phrases an author chooses to include in a text must be evaluated. How does the word choice affect the meaning and tone? By recognizing the use of literal and figurative language, a reader can more readily ascertain the message or purpose of a text. Literal word choice is the easiest to analyze as it represents the usual and intended way a word or phrase is used. It is also more common in informational texts because it is used to state facts and definitions. While figurative language is typically associated with fiction and poetry, it can be found in informational texts as well. The reader must determine not only what is meant by the figurative language in context, but also how the author intended it to shape the overall text.

Inference in Informational Text
Inference refers to the reader's ability to understand the unwritten text, i.e., "read between the lines" in terms of an author's intent or message. The strategy asks that a reader not take everything he or she reads at face value but instead, add his or her own interpretation of what the author seems to be trying to convey. A reader's ability to make inferences relies on his or her ability to think clearly and logically

about the text. It does not ask that the reader make wild speculation or guess about the material but demands that he or she be able to come to a sound conclusion about the material.

An author's use of less literal words and phrases requires readers to make more inference when they read. Since inference involves *deduction*—deriving conclusions from ideas assumed to be true—there's more room for interpretation. Still, critical readers who employ inference, if careful in their thinking, can still arrive at the logical, sound conclusions the author intends.

Textual Evidence in Informational Text
Once a reader has determined an author's thesis or main idea, he or she will need to understand how textual evidence supports interpretation of that thesis or main idea. Test takers will be asked direct questions regarding an author's main idea and may be asked to identify evidence that would support those ideas. This will require test takers to comprehend literal and figurative meanings within the text passage, be able to draw inferences from provided information, and be able to separate important evidence from minor supporting detail. It's often helpful to skim test questions and answer options prior to critically reading informational text; however, test takers should avoid the temptation to solely look for the correct answers. Just trying to find the "right answer" may cause test takers to miss important supporting textual evidence. Making mental note of test questions is only helpful as a guide when reading.

After identifying an author's thesis or main idea, a test taker should look at the supporting details that the author provides to back up his or her assertions, identifying those additional pieces of information that help expand the thesis. From there, test takers should examine that additional information and related details for credibility, the author's use of outside sources, and be able to point to direct evidence that supports the author's claims. It's also imperative that test takers be able to identify what is strong support and what is merely additional information that is nice to know but not necessary. Being able to make this differentiation will help test takers effectively answer questions regarding an author's use of supporting evidence within informational text.

Understanding Organizational Patterns and Structures
Organizational Structure within Informational Text
Informational text is specifically designed to relate factual information, and although it is open to a reader's interpretation and application of the facts, the structure of the presentation is carefully designed to lead the reader to a particular conclusion or central idea. When reading informational text, it is important that readers are able to understand its organizational structure as the structure often directly relates to an author's intent to inform and/or persuade the reader.

The first step in identifying the text's structure is to determine the thesis or main idea. The thesis statement and organization of a work are closely intertwined. *A thesis statement* indicates the writer's purpose and may include the scope and direction of the text. It may be presented at the beginning of a text or at the end, and it may be explicit or implicit.

Once a reader has a grasp of the thesis or main idea of the text, he or she can better determine its organizational structure. Test takers are advised to read informational text passages more than once in order to comprehend the material fully. It is also helpful to examine any text features present in the text including the table of contents, index, glossary, headings, footnotes, and visuals. The analysis of these features and the information presented within them, can offer additional clues about the central idea and structure of a text. The following questions should be asked when considering structure:

- How does the author assemble the parts to make an effective whole argument?
- Is the passage linear in nature and if so, what is the timeline or thread of logic?
- What is the presented order of events, facts, or arguments? Are these effective in contributing to the author's thesis?
- How can the passage be divided into sections? How are they related to each other and to the main idea or thesis?
- What key terms are used to indicate the organization?

Next, test takers should skim the passage, noting the first line or two of each body paragraph—the *topic sentences*—and the conclusion. Key *transitional terms*, such as *on the other hand, also, because, however, therefore, most importantly,* and *first,* within the text can also signal organizational structure. Based on these clues, readers should then be able to identify what type of organizational structure is being used. The following organizational structures are most common:

- *Problem/solution*—organized by an analysis/overview of a problem, followed by potential solution(s)

- *Cause/effect*—organized by the effects resulting from a cause or the cause(s) of a particular effect

- *Spatial order*—organized by points that suggest location or direction—e.g., top to bottom, right to left, outside to inside

- *Chronological/sequence order*—organized by points presented to indicate a passage of time or through purposeful steps/stages

- *Comparison/Contrast*—organized by points that indicate similarities and/or differences between two things or concepts

- *Order of importance*—organized by priority of points, often most significant to least significant or vice versa

Workplace and Community Documents
Workplace and *community* documents help employers to communicate within the business world and foster positive community relations outside of it. Workplace communications typically craft a specific message to a targeted audience while community documents send a broader or more generic message to a wider range of recipients.

Workplace Documents
Even though workplace-related documents are generated in a multitude of paper and electronic formats—memorandums, bulletin boards, presentations, web conferencing, instant messaging, and e-mails—in general all effective business communications share relevant information concisely, accurately, and purposefully. Supervisors rely on workplace documents to communicate expectations to

subordinates (downward communication), and subordinates rely on workplace documents to submit progress reports, ask questions, and address concerns with their supervisors (upward communication).

- Memorandums: Designed to communicate information to a wide audience, memorandums inform staff of company-wide policy changes. Similar to an e-mail, a memorandum has a header near the top which identifies the intended audience, the author of the memo, the subject of the memo, and the date it was issued. Unlike an e-mail, though, memorandums are longer, can be submitted in paper or electronic form, and contain an introduction that identifies the topic or problem, a body that expands on the topic, and a conclusion that suggests a course of action or solution.

- Bulletin Boards: Regardless of whether they are in paper or electronic form, bulletin boards provide a less formal setting for supervisors and staff to communicate. Bulletin boards are a perfect medium to post federal and state regulations, employee incentive initiatives, volunteer opportunities, and company news. While paper bulletin boards are limited to a specific office and personnel, electronic bulletin boards have the capability of broadcasting information nationally and even globally.

- Presentations: Presentations can be created with a variety of software—*PowerPoints*, *Google Slides*, and *Prezi*—and are given extemporaneously. Typically, presentations have an introductory slide, informational slides, and a concluding slide that gives the presenter's audience the opportunity to ask questions or create a dialogue. Presentations relay information in a media-rich format: graphics, tables, and hyperlinked documents and videos are easily imbedded within the slides.

- Web Conferencing: Web conferencing allows for employees to collaborate on projects and tasks. Employees are able to talk or videoconference from different locations, making it possible for remote workers from around the globe to participate simultaneously in one meeting. Web conferencing can be done via telephone with visuals (*PowerPoint* or *Microsoft Word* documents) or via video camera programs like *WebEx*®, *PGI GlobalMeet*®, and *Skype*®.

- Instant Messaging: Many staff outside of centralized locations who cannot communicate verbally with coworkers or supervisors rely, instead, on instant messaging programs. Instant messaging programs can deliver messages one-on-one or in circles and groups, and some software even provides screen-sharing capabilities. Since instant messaging is faster than e-mail, for many employees it has become the preferred method of communicating over long distances.

- E-Mails: In today's fast-paced business world, e-mails are heavily relied upon because they provide a platform that is perfect for quickly communicating brief, concise messages to targeted audiences. E-mails not only detail who the sender and receiver are but also provide a date, time, and subject line. Unlike a memorandum, sender and receiver can communicate back and forth, and, more importantly, they may do so over long distances. Many businesses today rely on *Google*, *Yahoo*, and *Outlook* mail severs.

Community Documents

Where business documents target a specific audience and often contain a higher level of proprietary, confidential, or sensitive information, community documents invite larger groups to discuss business matters in a less restrictive environment. Because community documents often help bridge the gap between businesses and community, an effective newsletter, discussion board, blog, website, and app have the power to influence public perception of private companies.

- Newsletters: Newsletters are used to provide the public information about the business. It can be used to generate excitement, inform or persuade staff or consumers, or give tips on how the public can contact or work with businesses. Newsletters can be mailed or sent electronically. Generally, newsletters are sent weekly, monthly, or quarterly. They can be interactive, providing the community a glance at what is going on with a business that they interact with, and, moreover, newsletters can communicate a company's mission, values, and priorities.

- Discussion Boards: Discussion boards offer a place to go to share information on a specific topic. Discussion boards are organized on menus, submenus, and discussion threads. People visit discussion boards to find out more about a topic. Discussion board members are granted greater access to the site and have greater power to publish and comment, but, still, visitors are welcome, and they often get difficult or obscure questions resolved.

- Blogs: A blog, which is usually centered on a specific topic or theme, is a website where individuals post and update information constantly. Blogs tend to feature the newest posts first while archiving older ones. Articles, editorials, images, videos, surveys, and social media (just to name a few) can all be imbedded within blogs. Menus, sidebars, recent posts, and search boxes help visitors wade through a dizzying array of media formats and topics. Though individuals can hire a web designer to create a blog for them, most people use existing platforms like *WordPress®, Blogger®*, and *Tumbler®*.

- Websites: As the world becomes more technologically savvy, a website can be used to house community documents, giving consumers instant access to tools they will need to interact with the business. It can house forms, contact information, discussion boards, surveys, and blogs. It is a one-stop-shop that can assist in the interaction between the business and the consumer. Websites are advantageous because they can be accessed via computer, tablet, or mobile phone.

- Apps: Similar to a website, an application (app) gives businesses yet another method to reach individuals or segments of a community. Apps provide instant access to forms and other documentation. Designed to be downloaded on tablets or mobile phones, apps are streamlined and intuitive, allowing consumers on the go to access information at their convenience. The primary operating systems for apps include *iOS®* and *Android®*.

Identifying Primary Sources in Various Media

Primary sources are best defined as records or items that serve as evidence of periods of history. To be considered primary, the source documents or objects must have been created during the time period in which they reference. Examples include diaries, newspaper articles, speeches, government documents, photographs, and historical artifacts. In today's digital age, primary sources, which were once in print, often are embedded in secondary sources. Secondary sources, such as websites, history books, databases, or reviews, contain analysis or commentary on primary sources. Secondary sources borrow information from primary sources through the process of quoting, summarizing, or paraphrasing.

Today's students often complete research online through electronic sources. Electronic sources offer advantages over print, and can be accessed on virtually any computer, where libraries or other research centers are limited to fixed locations and specific catalogs. Electronic sources also are efficient and yield massive amounts of data in seconds. The user can tailor a search based on key words, publication years, and article length. Lastly, many databases provide the user with instant citations, saving the user the trouble of manually assembling sources.

Though electronic sources yield powerful results, researchers must use caution. While there are many reputable and reliable sources on the internet, just as many are unreliable or biased sources. It's up to the researcher to examine and verify the reliability of sources. *Wikipedia*, for example, may or may not be accurate, depending on the contributor. Many databases, such as *EBSCO* or *SIRS*, offer peer reviewed articles, meaning the publications have been reviewed for the quality of their content.

Evaluating an Argument and its Specific Claims

It's important to evaluate the author's supporting details to be sure that the details are credible, provide evidence of the author's point, and directly support the main idea. Though shocking statistics grab readers' attention, their use could be ineffective information in the piece. Details like this are crucial to understanding the passage and evaluating how well the author presents their argument and evidence.

Readers draw **conclusions** about what an author has presented. This helps them better understand what the writer has intended to communicate and whether they agree with what the author has offered (or not). There are a few ways to determine a logical conclusion, but careful reading is the most important. It's helpful to read a passage a few times, noting details that seem important to the piece. Sometimes, readers arrive at a conclusion that is different than what the writer intended or come up with more than one conclusion.

Evidence

It is important to distinguish between *fact and opinion* when reading a piece of writing. When an author presents *facts*, such as statistics or data, readers should be able to check those facts and make sure they are accurate. When authors use *opinion*, they are sharing their own thoughts and feelings about a subject.

Textual evidence within the details helps readers draw a conclusion about a passage. *Textual evidence* refers to information—facts and examples that support the main point. Textual evidence will likely come from outside sources and can be in the form of quoted or paraphrased material. In order to draw a conclusion from evidence, it's important to examine the credibility and validity of that evidence as well as how (and if) it relates to the main idea.

Credibility

Critical readers examine the facts used to support an author's argument. They check the facts against other sources to be sure those facts are correct. They also check the validity of the sources used to be sure those sources are credible, academic, and/or peer- reviewed. Consider that when an author uses another person's opinion to support their argument, even if it is an expert's opinion, it is still only an opinion and should not be taken as fact. A strong argument uses valid, measurable facts to support ideas. Even then, the reader may disagree with the argument as it may be rooted in their personal beliefs.

An authoritative argument may use the facts to sway the reader. In the example of global warming, many experts differ in their opinions of what alternative fuels can be used to aid in offsetting it. Because of this, a writer may choose to only use the information and expert opinion that supports their viewpoint.

Appeal to Emotion

An author's argument might also appeal to readers' emotions, perhaps by including personal stories and *anecdotes* (a short narrative of a specific event).

The next example presents an appeal to emotion. By sharing the personal anecdote of one student and speaking about emotional topics like family relationships, the author invokes the reader's empathy in asking them to reconsider the school rule.

> Our school should abolish its current ban on cell phone use on campus. If they aren't able to use their phones during the school day, many students feel isolated from their loved ones. For example, last semester, one student's grandmother had a heart attack in the morning. However, because he couldn't use his cell phone, the student didn't know about his grandmother's accident until the end of the day—when she had already passed away and it was too late to say goodbye. By preventing students from contacting their friends and family, our school is placing undue stress and anxiety on students.

Counter-Arguments

If an author presents a differing opinion or a *counter-argument* in order to refute it, the reader should consider how and why this information is being presented. It is meant to strengthen the original argument and shouldn't be confused with the author's intended conclusion, but it should also be considered in the reader's final evaluation. On the contrary, sometimes authors will concede to an opposing argument by recognizing the validity the other side has to offer. A concession will allow readers to see both sides of the argument in an unbiased light, thereby increasing the credibility of the author.

Authors can also reflect **bias** if they ignore an opposing viewpoint or present their side in an unbalanced way. A strong argument considers the opposition and finds a way to refute it. Critical readers should look for an unfair or one-sided presentation of the argument and be skeptical, as a bias may be present. Even if this bias is unintentional, if it exists in the writing, the reader should be wary of the validity of the argument.

Revising/Editing

Nouns

A noun is a person, place, thing, or idea. All nouns fit into one of two types, common or proper.

A *common noun* is a word that identifies any of a class of people, places, or things. Examples include numbers, objects, animals, feelings, concepts, qualities, and actions. *A, an,* or *the* usually precedes the common noun. These parts of speech are called *articles*. Here are some examples of sentences using nouns preceded by articles.

A building is under construction.
The girl would like to move to *the* city.

A *proper noun* (also called a *proper name*) is used for the specific name of an individual person, place, or organization. The first letter in a proper noun is capitalized. "My name is *Mary*." "I work for *Walmart*."

Nouns sometimes serve as adjectives (which themselves describe nouns), such as "hockey player" and "state government."

Pronouns

A word used in place of a noun is known as a *pronoun*. Pronouns are words like *I, mine, hers,* and *us*.

Pronouns can be split into different classifications (seen below) which make them easier to learn; however, it's not important to memorize the classifications.

- Personal pronouns: refer to people
  - First person: we, I, our, mine
  - Second person: you, yours
  - Third person: he, them
- Possessive pronouns: demonstrate ownership (mine, my, his, yours)
- Interrogative pronouns: ask questions (what, which, who, whom, whose)
- Relative pronouns: include the five interrogative pronouns and others that are relative (whoever, whomever, that, when, where)
- Demonstrative pronouns: replace something specific (this, that, those, these)
- Reciprocal pronouns: indicate something was done or given in return (each other, one another)
- Indefinite pronouns: have a nonspecific status (anybody, whoever, someone, everybody, somebody)

Indefinite pronouns such as *anybody, whoever, someone, everybody*, and *somebody* command a singular verb form, but others such as *all, none,* and *some* could require a singular or plural verb form.

Antecedents

An *antecedent* is the noun to which a pronoun refers; it needs to be written or spoken before the pronoun is used. For many pronouns, antecedents are imperative for clarity. In particular, a lot of the personal, possessive, and demonstrative pronouns need antecedents. Otherwise, it would be unclear who or what someone is referring to when they use a pronoun like *he* or *this*.

Pronoun reference means that the pronoun should refer clearly to one, clear, unmistakable noun (the antecedent).

Pronoun-antecedent agreement refers to the need for the antecedent and the corresponding pronoun to agree in gender, person, and number. Here are some examples:

The *kidneys* (plural antecedent) are part of the urinary system. *They* (plural pronoun) serve several roles."

The kidneys are part of the *urinary system* (singular antecedent). *It* (singular pronoun) is also known as the renal system.

Pronoun Cases

The subjective pronouns —*I, you, he/she/it, we, they,* and *who*—are the subjects of the sentence.

Example: *They* have a new house.

The objective pronouns—*me, you* (*singular*)*, him/her, us, them,* and *whom*—are used when something is being done for or given to someone; they are objects of the action.

> Example: The teacher has an apple for *us*.

The possessive pronouns—*mine, my, your, yours, his, hers, its, their, theirs, our,* and *ours*—are used to denote that something (or someone) belongs to someone (or something).

> Example: It's *their* chocolate cake.
> Even Better Example: It's *my* chocolate cake!

One of the greatest challenges and worst abuses of pronouns concerns *who* and *whom*. Just knowing the following rule can eliminate confusion. *Who* is a subjective-case pronoun used only as a subject or subject complement. *Whom* is only objective-case and, therefore, the object of the verb or preposition.

> *Who* is going to the concert?

> You are going to the concert with *whom*?

Hint: When using *who* or *whom*, think of whether someone would say *he* or *him*. If the answer is *he*, use *who*. If the answer is *him*, use *whom*. This trick is easy to remember because *he* and *who* both end in vowels, and *him* and *whom* both end in the letter *M*.

Adjectives

"The *extraordinary* brain is the *main* organ of the central nervous system." The adjective *extraordinary* describes the brain in a way that causes one to realize it is more exceptional than some of other organs while the adjective *main* defines the brain's importance in its system.

An *adjective* is a word or phrase that names an attribute that describes or clarifies a noun or pronoun. This helps the reader visualize and understand the characteristics—size, shape, age, color, origin, etc.—of a person, place, or thing that otherwise might not be known. Adjectives breathe life, color, and depth into the subjects they define. Life would be *drab* and *colorless* without adjectives!

Adjectives often precede the nouns they describe.

> *She drove her <u>new</u> car.*

However, adjectives can also come later in the sentence.

> *Her car is <u>new</u>.*

Adjectives using the prefix *a–* can only be used after a verb.

> Correct: The dog was alive until the car ran up on the curb and hit him.
> Incorrect: The alive dog was hit by a car that ran up on the curb.

Other examples of this rule include *awake, ablaze, ajar, alike,* and *asleep.*

Other adjectives used after verbs concern states of health.

> The girl was finally *well* after a long bout of pneumonia.
> The boy was *fine* after the accident.

An adjective phrase is not a bunch of adjectives strung together, but a group of words that describes a noun or pronoun and, thus, functions as an adjective. *Very ugly* is an adjective phrase; so are *way too fat* and *faster than a speeding bullet.*

Possessives

In grammar, *possessive nouns* show ownership, which was seen in previous examples like *mine, yours,* and *theirs.*

Singular nouns are generally made possessive with an apostrophe and an *s* (*'s*).

> My *uncle's* new car is silver.
> The *dog's* bowl is empty.
> *James's* ties are becoming outdated.

Plural nouns ending in *s* are generally made possessive by just adding an apostrophe (*'*):

> The pistachio nuts' saltiness is added during roasting. (The saltiness of pistachio nuts is added during roasting.)
> The students' achievement tests are difficult. (The achievement tests of the students are difficult.)

If the plural noun does not end in an *s* such as *women,* then it is made possessive by adding an *apostrophe s* (*'s*)—*women's.*

Indefinite possessive pronouns such as *nobody* or *someone* become possessive by adding an *apostrophe s*— *nobody's* or *someone's.*

Verbs

The *verb* is the part of speech that describes an action, state of being, or occurrence.

A *verb* forms the main part of a predicate of a sentence. This means that the verb explains what the noun (which will be discussed shortly) is doing. A simple example is *time <u>flies</u>.* The verb *flies* explains what the action of the noun, *time,* is doing. This example is a *main* verb.

Helping (auxiliary) verbs are words like *have, do, be, can, may, should, must,* and *will.* "I *should* go to the store." Helping verbs assist main verbs in expressing tense, ability, possibility, permission, or obligation.

Particles are minor function words like *not, in, out, up,* or *down* that become part of the verb itself. "I might *not.*"

Participles are words formed from verbs that are often used to modify a noun, noun phrase, verb, or verb phrase.

> The *running* teenager collided with the cyclist.

Participles can also create compound verb forms.

> He is *speaking.*

Verbs have five basic forms: the *base* form, the *-s* form, the *-ing* form, the *past* form, and the *past participle* form.

The *past* forms are either *regular* (*love/loved; hate/hated*) or *irregular* because they don't end by adding the common past tense suffix "-ed" (*go/went; fall/fell; set/set*).

Adverbs

Adverbs have more functions than adjectives because they modify or qualify verbs, adjectives, or other adverbs as well as word groups that express a relation of place, time, circumstance, or cause. Therefore, adverbs answer any of the following questions: *How, when, where, why, in what way, how often, how much, in what condition,* and/or *to what degree. How good looking is he? He is <u>very</u> handsome.*

Here are some examples of adverbs for different situations:

- how: quickly
- when: daily
- where: there
- in what way: easily
- how often: often
- how much: much
- in what condition: badly
- what degree: hardly

As one can see, for some reason, many adverbs end in *-ly.*

Adverbs do things like emphasize (*really, simply,* and *so*), amplify (*heartily, completely,* and *positively*), and tone down (*almost, somewhat,* and *mildly*).

Adverbs also come in phrases.

> The dog ran as <u>though his life depended on it.</u>

Prepositions

Prepositions are connecting words and, while there are only about 150 of them, they are used more often than any other individual groups of words. They describe relationships between other words. They are placed before a noun or pronoun, forming a phrase that modifies another word in the sentence. *Prepositional phrases* begin with a preposition and end with a noun or pronoun, the *object of the preposition. A pristine lake is <u>near the store</u> and <u>behind the bank</u>.*

Some commonly used prepositions are *about, after, anti, around, as, at, behind, beside, by, for, from, in, into, of, off, on, to,* and *with.*

Complex prepositions, which also come before a noun or pronoun, consist of two or three words such as *according to, in regards to,* and *because of.*

Interjections

Interjections are words used to express emotion. Examples include *wow, ouch,* and *hooray.* Interjections are often separate from sentences; in those cases, the interjection is directly followed by an exclamation point. In other cases the interjection is included in a sentence and followed by a comma. The punctuation plays a big role in the intensity of the emotion that the interjection is expressing. Using a comma or semicolon indicates less excitement than using an exclamation mark

Conjunctions

Conjunctions are vital words that connect words, phrases, thoughts, and ideas. Conjunctions show relationships between components. There are two types:

Coordinating conjunctions are the primary class of conjunctions placed between words, phrases, clauses, and sentences that are of equal grammatical rank; the coordinating conjunctions are for, and, nor, but, or, yes, and so. A useful memorization trick is to remember that the first letter of these conjunctions collectively spell the word *fanboys*.

> I need to go shopping, *but* I must be careful to leave enough money in the bank.
> She wore a black, red, *and* white shirt.

Subordinating conjunctions are the secondary class of conjunctions. They connect two unequal parts, one *main* (or *independent*) and the other *subordinate* (or *dependent*). I must go to the store *even though* I do not have enough money in the bank.

> *Because* I read the review, I do not want to go to the movie.

Notice that the presence of subordinating conjunctions makes clauses dependent. *I read the review* is an independent clause, but *because* makes the clause dependent. Thus, it needs an independent clause to complete the sentence.

Subject-Verb Agreement

The subject of a sentence and its verb must agree. The cornerstone rule of subject-verb agreement is that subject and verb must agree in number. Whether the subject is singular or plural, the verb must follow suit.

> Incorrect: The houses is new.
> Correct: The houses are new.
> Also Correct: The house is new.

In other words, a singular subject requires a singular verb; a plural subject requires a plural verb. The words or phrases that come between the subject and verb do not alter this rule.

> Incorrect: The houses built of brick is new.
> Correct: The houses built of brick are new.

> Incorrect: The houses with the sturdy porches is new.
> Correct: The houses with the sturdy porches are new.

The subject will always follow the verb when a sentence begins with *here* or *there*. Identify these with care.

> Incorrect: Here *is* the *houses* with sturdy porches.
> Correct: Here *are* the *houses* with sturdy porches.

The subject in the sentences above is not *here*, it is *houses*. Remember, *here* and *there* are never subjects. Be careful that contractions such as *here's* or *there're* do not cause confusion!

Two subjects joined by *and* require a plural verb form, except when the two combine to make one thing:

> Incorrect: Garrett and Jonathan is over there.
> Correct: Garrett and Jonathan are over there.
>
> Incorrect: Spaghetti and meatballs are a delicious meall
> Correct: Spaghetti and meatballs is a delicious meal!

In the example above, *spaghetti and meatballs* is a compound noun. However, *Garrett and Jonathan* is not a compound noun.

Two singular subjects joined by *or, either/or,* or *neither/nor* call for a singular verb form.

> Incorrect: Butter or syrup are acceptable.
> Correct: Butter or syrup is acceptable.

Plural subjects joined by *or, either/or,* or *neither/nor* are, indeed, plural.

> The chairs or the boxes are being moved next.

If one subject is singular and the other is plural, the verb should agree with the closest noun.

> Correct: The chair or the boxes are being moved next.
> Correct: The chairs or the box is being moved next.

Some plurals of money, distance, and time call for a singular verb.

> Incorrect: Three dollars *are* enough to buy that.
> Correct: Three dollars *is* enough to buy that.

For words declaring degrees of quantity such as *many of, some of,* or *most of,* let the noun that follows *of* be the guide:

> Incorrect: Many of the books is in the shelf.
> Correct: Many of the books are in the shelf.
>
> Incorrect: Most of the pie *are* on the table.
> Correct: Most of the pie *is* on the table.

For indefinite pronouns like anybody or everybody, use singular verbs.

> Everybody *is* going to the store.

However, the pronouns *few, many, several, all, some,* and *both* have their own rules and use plural forms.

> Some *are* ready.

Some nouns like *crowd* and *congress* are called *collective nouns* and they require a singular verb form.

> Congress *is* in session.
> The news *is* over.

Books and movie titles, though, including plural nouns such as *Great Expectations*, also require a singular verb. Remember that only the subject affects the verb. While writing tricky subject-verb arrangements, say them aloud. Listen to them. Once the rules have been learned, one's ear will become sensitive to them, making it easier to pick out what's right and what's wrong.

Independent and Dependent Clauses

Independent and *dependent* clauses are strings of words that contain both a subject and a verb. An independent clause *can* stand alone as complete thought, but a dependent clause *cannot*. A dependent clause relies on other words to be a complete sentence.

> Independent clause: The keys are on the counter.
> Dependent clause: If the keys are on the counter

Notice that both clauses have a subject (*keys*) and a verb (*are*). The independent clause expresses a complete thought, but the word *if* at the beginning of the dependent clause makes it *dependent* on other words to be a complete thought.

> Independent clause: If the keys are on the counter, please give them to me.

This presents a complete sentence since it includes at least one verb and one subject and is a complete thought. In this case, the independent clause has two subjects (*keys* & an implied *you*) and two verbs (*are* & *give*).

> Independent clause: I went to the store.
> Dependent clause: Because we are out of milk,
>
> Complete Sentence: Because we are out of milk, I went to the store.
> Complete Sentence: I went to the store because we are out of milk.

A *phrase* is a group of words that does not contain both a subject and a verb.

Active and Passive Voice

Active voice is a sentence structure in which the subject performs the action of the sentence. The verbs of these sentences are called *active verbs*.

> The deer jumped over the fence.

In the example above, the deer is the one jumping. *Passive voice* is a sentence structure in which the object performs the action of the sentence. The verbs of these sentences are called *passive verbs*.

> The fence was jumped by the deer.

In this example, the fence is the subject, but it is not jumping over anything. The deer is still the one performing the action, but it is now the object of the sentence.

Passive voice is helpful when it's unclear who performed an action.

> The chair was moved.

While passive voice can add variety to writing, active voice is the generally preferred sentence structure.

Dialogue

Dialogue is a literary device that writers use to show conversations between characters in their stories, books, movies, plays, or other original works.

> "Will you go to the store with me?" the young man asked his brother.

Quotation marks written immediately before the beginning and immediately after the end of a statement indicate that these are the exact words spoken or written by someone. They are, thus, a *quote*. Be sure to place the period or comma within the quotations. The comma is used if the author plans to continue writing.

> Jackie said, "Get some potatoes at the store."
> Jackie said, "Get some potatoes at the store," as she ended the phone call.

Question marks and exclamation points should also go inside quotations if they are part of the quotation.

> Jackie asked, "Will you get me some potatoes at the store?" and I responded, "Of course I will."
> Was it Jackie that said, "Get some potatoes at the store"?

Quotation marks may also be used to express the unspoken thoughts of a character. An alternative to this is to italicize this type of dialogue.

> "I'm so lucky to have such a great sister," thought Sherri.
> *I'm so lucky to have such a great sister,* thought Sherri.

When a quote is used within a quote, just a single quotation mark (looks like the apostrophe ') is used.

> "Why did Mrs. Adkins say 'You need be a better team player,' when you were the one that did all of the work on the group project?" Derek asked.

Narrative Voice

An important aspect of writing to keep in mind is perspective. Is it *first* person, *second* person, *third* person, or written from *multiple* points of view?

1st Person
Writing from the *first person* perspective means that the *"I"* or *"me"* of a composition is the main character, narrator, or storyteller. Many challenges are inherent in writing from this perspective, including keeping the audience's attention. How well does that work for someone when he or she is talking? Does it sound like a repetitive "I"? If so, after a while, it's easy for the audience to tune the speaker out. Creativity and knowledge takes a vital role when writing in the first person. Of course, this depends entirely on what genre the writing is and the level of interest in the story.

2nd Person

The *second person* perspective uses the pronoun *"you," "your,"* and *"yours,"* and with it, the author can draw the reader in because he or she is speaking directly to him or her. This perspective is effectively used in advertising, counsel, directions, technical writing, and speeches, provided the author knows his or her audience. Tone also has a pronounced effect in second person. Is the tone accusatory or loving? Is it commanding or counseling?'

3rd Person

Writing in the *third person* calls for the use of pronouns: *he, she, it,* and *they.* Third person is often used for fiction and academics. The third person perspective presents the author with the opportunity to write as one who is omniscient because, writing on behalf of others, he or she can know everything about them and all that's transpiring.

Multiple Points of View

Writing in *multiple points of view* might sound overwhelming. Well, okay, it probably is, but it can be worth it. Many successful novels are written using multiple perspectives. Obviously, great care with structure and continuity is required as one transitions between the points of view.

Context Clues

Context clues help readers understand unfamiliar words, and thankfully, there are many types.

Synonyms are words or phrases that have nearly, if not exactly, the same meaning as other words or phrases

> *Large* boxes are needed to pack *big* items.

Antonyms are words or phrases that have opposite definitions. Antonyms, like synonyms, can serve as context clues, although more cryptically.

> *Large* boxes are not needed to pack *small* items.

Definitions are sometimes included within a sentence to define uncommon words.

> They practiced the *rumba*, a *type of dance*, for hours on end.

Explanations provide context through elaboration.

> Large boxes holding items weighing over 60 pounds were stacked in the corner.

Here's an example of *contrast*:

> These *minute* creatures were much different than the *huge* mammals that the zoologist was accustomed to dealing with.

Word Usage

Word usage: the way and manner in which writers choose to use words (or phrases). This is a vital consideration in order to create excellence in writing. Context plays a role in the selection of words, as does simple choice.

Correct word usage can be as basic and imperative as making the right grammatical choice.

> Incorrect: I never *seen* that play
> Correct: I never *saw* that play.

Seen (past participle of see) in place of *saw* (the correct past tense of *see*) is a relatively common and grievous mistake.

> Incorrect: *There* going to the store with *there* parents.
> Correct: *They're* going to the store with *their* parents.

There (adverb) mistaken for *they're* (contraction for "they are") and *there* (adverb) for *their* (pronoun) are also frequent grammatical errors.

Correct word usage can be as simple as choosing between synonyms. For instance, determining whether to say *for instance* or *for example*! Would it be better to use the word *incongruous* or *inappropriate* for *unsuited,* or when the woman is *uncouth,* would *redneck, uninformed,* or *illiterate* better define her?

Correct word usage can also be as simple as knowing how to access and make good use of dictionaries, thesauruses, grammar correction software, and search engines on computers, tablets, and smartphones.

Word Parts

By analyzing and understanding Latin, Greek, and Anglo-Saxon word roots, prefixes, and suffixes one can better understand word meanings. Of course, people can always look words up if a dictionary or thesaurus if available, but meaning can often be gleaned on the spot if the writer learns to dissect and examine words.

A word can consist of the following:

- root
- root + suffix
- prefix + root
- prefix + root + suffix

For example, if someone was unfamiliar with the word *submarine* they could break the word into its parts.

> prefix + root
> sub + marine

It can be determined that *sub* means *below* as in *subway* and *subpar.* Additionally, one can determine that *marine* refers to *the sea* as in *marine life.* Thus, it can be figured that *submarine* refers to something below the water.

Roots

Roots are the basic components of words. Many roots can stand alone as individual words, but others must be combined with a prefix or suffix to be a word. For example, *calc* is a root but it needs a suffix to be an actual word (*calcium*).

Prefixes

A *prefix* is a word, letter, or number that is placed before another. It adjusts or qualifies the root word's meaning. When written alone, prefixes are followed by a dash to indicate that the root word follows. Some of the most common prefixes are the following:

Prefix	Meaning	Example
dis-	not or opposite of	disabled
in-, im-, il-, ir-	not	illiterate
re-	again	return
un-	not	unpredictable
anti-	against	antibacterial
fore-	before	forefront
mis-	wrongly	misunderstand
non-	not	nonsense
over-	more than normal	overabundance
pre-	before	preheat
super-	above	superman

Suffixes

A suffix is a letter or group of letters added at the end of a word to form another word. The word created from the root and suffix is either a different tense of the same root (*help* + *ed* = *helped*) or a new word (*help* + *ful* = *helpful*). When written alone, suffixes are preceded by a dash to indicate that the root word comes before.

Some of the most common suffixes are the following:

Suffix	Meaning	Example
ed	makes a verb past tense	wash*ed*
ing	makes a verb a present participle verb	wash*ing*
ly	to make characteristic of	love*ly*
s/es	to make more than one	chair*s*, box*es*
able	can be done	deplor*able*
al	having characteristics of	comic*al*
est	comparative	great*est*
ful	full of	wonder*ful*
ism	belief in	commun*ism*
less	without	faith*less*
ment	action or process	accomplish*ment*
ness	state of	happi*ness*
ize, ise	to render, to make	steril*ize*, advert*ise*
cede/ceed/sede	go	con*cede*, pro*ceed*, super*sede*

Here are some helpful tips:

- When adding a suffix that starts with a vowel (for example, *-ed*) to a one-syllable root whose vowel has a short sound and ends in a consonant (for example, *stun*), double the final consonant of the root (*n*).

    stun + ed = stun*n*ed

    Exception: If the past tense verb ends in *x* such as *box*, do not double the *x*.

    box + ed = boxed

- If adding a suffix that starts with a vowel (*-er*) to a multi-syllable word ending in a consonant (*begin*), double the consonant (*n*).

    begin + er = begin*n*er

- If a short vowel is followed by two or more consonants in a word such as *i+t+c+h = itch*, do <u>not</u> double the last consonant.

    itch + ed = itched

- If adding a suffix that starts with a vowel (*-ing*) to a word ending in *e* (for example, *name*), that word's final *e* is generally (but not always) dropped.

    name + ing = naming
    exception: manage + able = manag*e*able

- If adding a suffix that starts with a consonant (-*ness*) to a word ending in *e* (*complete*), the *e* generally (but not always) remains.

> complete + ness = completeness
> exception: judge + ment = judgment

There is great diversity on handling words that end in *y*. For words ending in a vowel + y, nothing changes in the original word.

> play + ed = played

For words ending in a consonant + y, change the *y* to *i* when adding any suffix except for *–ing*.

> marry + ed = married
> marry + ing = marrying

Sentence Fluency

It's time to take what's been studied and put it all together in order to construct well-written sentences and paragraphs that have correct structure. Learning and utilizing the mechanics of structure will encourage effective, professional results, and adding some creativity will elevate one's writing to a higher level.

First, let's review the basic elements of sentences.

A *sentence* is a set of words that make up a grammatical unit. The words must have certain elements and be spoken or written in a specific order to constitute a complete sentence that makes sense.

> 1. A sentence must have a *subject* (a noun or noun phrase). The subject tells whom or what the sentence is addressing (i.e. what it is about).

> 2. A sentence must have an *action* or *state of being* (*a verb*). To reiterate: A verb forms the main part of the predicate of a sentence. This means that it explains what the noun is doing.

> 3. A sentence must convey a complete thought.

When examining writing, be mindful of grammar, structure, spelling, and patterns. Sentences can come in varying sizes and shapes; so, the point of grammatical correctness is not to stamp out creativity or diversity in writing. Rather, grammatical correctness ensures that writing will be enjoyable and clear. One of the most common methods for catching errors is to mouth the words as you read them. Many typos are fixed automatically by our brain, but mouthing the words often circumvents this instinct and helps one read what's actually on the page. Often, grammar errors are caught not by memorization of grammar rules but by the training of one's mind to know whether something *sounds* right or not.

Types of Sentences

There isn't an overabundance of absolutes in grammar, but here is one: every sentence in the English language falls into one of four categories.

- Declarative: a simple statement that ends with a period

> The price of milk per gallon is the same as the price of gasoline.

- Imperative: a command, instruction, or request that ends with a period

    Buy milk when you stop to fill up your car with gas.

- Interrogative: a question that ends with a question mark

    Will you buy the milk?

- Exclamatory: a statement or command that expresses emotions like anger, urgency, or surprise and ends with an exclamation mark

    Buy the milk now!

Declarative sentences are the most common type, probably because they are comprised of the most general content, without any of the bells and whistles that the other three types contain. They are, simply, declarations or statements of any degree of seriousness, importance, or information.

Imperative sentences often seem to be missing a subject. The subject is there, though; it is just not visible or audible because it is *implied*. Look at the imperative example sentence.

    Buy the milk when you fill up your car with gas.

You is the implied subject, the one to whom the command is issued. This is sometimes called *the understood you* because it is understood that *you* is the subject of the sentence.

Interrogative sentences—those that ask questions—are defined as such from the idea of the word *interrogation*, the action of questions being asked of suspects by investigators. Although that is serious business, interrogative sentences apply to all kinds of questions.

To exclaim is at the root of *exclamatory* sentences. These are made with strong emotions behind them. The only technical difference between a declarative or imperative sentence and an exclamatory one is the exclamation mark at the end. The example declarative and imperative sentences can both become an exclamatory one simply by putting an exclamation mark at the end of the sentences.

    The price of milk per gallon is the same as the price of gasoline!
    Buy milk when you stop to fill up your car with gas!

After all, someone might be really excited by the price of gas or milk, or they could be mad at the person that will be buying the milk! However, as stated before, exclamation marks in abundance defeat their own purpose! After a while, they begin to cause fatigue! When used only for their intended purpose, they can have their expected and desired effect.

Lengths

The ideal sentence length—the number of words in a sentence—depends upon the sentence's purpose.

It's okay for a sentence to be brief, and it's fine for a sentence to be lengthy. It's just important to make sure that long sentences do not become run-on sentences or too long to keep up with.

To keep writing interesting, vary sentence lengths, using a mixture of short, medium and long sentences.

Transitions

Transitions are the glue use to make organized thoughts adhere to one another. Transitions are the glue that helps put ideas together seamlessly, within sentences and paragraphs, between them, and (in longer documents) even between sections. Transitions may be single words, sentences, or whole paragraphs (as in the prior example). Transitions help readers to digest and understand what to feel about what has gone on and clue readers in on what is going on, what will be, and how they might react to all these factors. Transitions are like good clues left at a crime scene.

Parallel Structure in a Sentence

Parallel structure, also known as parallelism, refers to using the same grammatical form within a sentence. This is important in lists and for other components of sentences.

> Incorrect: At the recital, the boys and girls were dancing, singing, and played musical instruments.
> Correct: At the recital, the boys and girls were dancing, singing, and playing musical instruments.

Notice that in the second example, *played* is not in the same verb tense as the other verbs nor is it compatible with the helping verb *were*. To test for parallel structure in lists, try reading each item as if it were the only item in the list.

> The boys and girls were dancing.
> The boys and girls were singing.
> The boys and girls were played musical instruments.

Suddenly, the error in the sentence becomes very clear. Here's another example:

> Incorrect: After the accident, I informed the police *that Mrs. Holmes backed* into my car, *that Mrs. Holmes got out* of her car to look at the damage, and *she was driving* off without leaving a note.

> Correct: After the accident, I informed the police *that Mrs. Holmes backed* into my car, *that Mrs. Holmes got out* of her car to look at the damage, and *that Mrs. Holmes drove off* without leaving a note.

> Correct: After the accident, I informed the police that Mrs. Holmes *backed* into my car, *got out* of her car to look at the damage, and *drove off* without leaving a note.

Note that there are two ways to fix the nonparallel structure of the first sentence. The key to parallelism is consistent structure.

Examples of Transitional Words and Phrases

Transitions have many emphases as can be seen below.

- To show emphasis: truly, in fact
- To show examples: for example, namely, specifically
- To show similarities: also, likewise
- To show dissimilarities: on the other hand, even if, in contrast
- To show progression of time: later, previously, subsequently

- To show sequence or order: next, finally
- To show cause and effect: therefore, so
- To show place or position: above, nearby, there
- To provide evidence: furthermore, then
- To summarize: finally, summarizing

Sentence Structures

- Simple sentence: composed of one independent clause

   Many people watch hummingbirds.

Note that it has one subject and one verb; however, a simple sentence can have a compound subject and/or a compound verb.

   Adults and children often enjoy watching and photographing hummingbirds.

- Compound sentence: composed of two independent clauses

   The wind knocked down lots of trees, but no trees in my yard were affected.

- Complex sentence: composed of one independent clause and one dependent clause

   Although the wind knocked down lots of trees, no trees in my yard were affected.

Forming Paragraphs

A good *paragraph* should have the following characteristics:

- Be logical with organized sentences
- Have a *unified* purpose within itself
- Use sentences as *building blocks*
- Be a *distinct section* of a piece of writing
- Present a *single theme* introduced by a *topic sentence*
- Maintain a *consistent flow* through subsequent, relevant, well-placed sentences
- *Tell a story* of its own or have its own purpose, yet connect with what is written before and after
- *Enlighten, entertain,* and/or *inform*

Though certainly not set in stone, the length should be a consideration for the reader's sake, not merely for the sake of the topic. When paragraphs are especially short, the reader might experience an irregular, uneven effect; when they're much longer than 250 words, the reader's attention span, and probably their retention, is challenged. While a paragraph can technically be a sentence long, a good rule of thumb is for paragraphs to be at least three sentences long and no more than ten sentence long. An optimal word length is 100 to 250 words.

Coherent Paragraphs

Coherence is simply defined as the quality of being logical and consistent. In order to have coherent paragraphs, therefore, authors must be logical and consistent in their writing, whatever the document might be. Two words are helpful to understanding coherence: flow and relationship. Earlier, transitions were referred to as being the "glue" to put organized thoughts together. Now, let's look at the topic sentence from which flow and relationship originate.

The topic sentence, usually the first in a paragraph, holds the essential features that will be brought forth in the paragraph. It is also here that authors either grab or lose readers. It may be the only writing that a reader encounters from that writer, so it is a good idea to summarize and represent ideas accurately.

The coherent paragraph has a logical order. It utilizes transitional words and phrases, parallel sentence structure, clear pronoun references, and reasonable repetition of key words and phrases. Use common sense for repetition. Consider synonyms for variety. Be consistent in verb tense whenever possible.

When writers have accomplished their paragraph's purpose, they prepare it to receive the next paragraph. While writing, read the paragraph over, edit, examine, evaluate, and make changes accordingly. Possibly, a paragraph has gone on too long. If that occurs, it needs to be broken up into other paragraphs, or the length should be reduced. If a paragraph didn't fully accomplish its purpose, consider revising it.

Simple Sentences

A *simple sentence* has one independent clause.

>   I am going to win.

A *compound sentence* has two independent clauses. A conjunction—*for, and, nor, but, or, yet, so*—links them together. Note that each of the independent clauses has a subject and a verb.

>   I am going to win, but the odds are against me.

A *complex sentence* has one independent clause and one or more dependent clauses.

>   I am going to win, even though I don't deserve it.

Even though I don't deserve it is a dependent clause. It does not stand on its own. Some conjunctions that link an independent and a dependent clause are *although, because, before, after, that, when, which,* and *while.*

A *compound-complex sentence* has at least three clauses, two of which are independent and at least one that is a dependent clause.

While trying to dance, I tripped over my partner's feet, but I regained my balance quickly.

>   The dependent clause is *While trying to dance.*

Practice Questions

Editing/Revising

1. What is the structure of the following sentence?

    The restaurant is unconventional because it serves both Chicago style pizza and New York style pizza.

    a. Simple
    b. Compound
    c. Complex
    d. Compound-complex

2. The following sentence contains what kind of error?

    This summer, I'm planning to travel to Italy, take a Mediterranean cruise, going to Pompeii, and eat a lot of Italian food.

    a. Parallelism
    b. Sentence fragment
    c. Misplaced modifier
    d. Subject-verb agreement

3. The following sentence contains what kind of error?

    Forgetting that he was supposed to meet his girlfriend for dinner, Anita was mad when Fred showed up late.

    a. Parallelism
    b. Run-on sentence
    c. Misplaced modifier
    d. Subject-verb agreement

4. The following sentence contains what kind of error?

    Some workers use all their sick leave, other workers cash out their leave.

    a. Parallelism
    b. Comma splice
    c. Sentence fragment
    d. Subject-verb agreement

5. A student writes the following in an essay:

> Protestors filled the streets of the city. Because they were dissatisfied with the government's leadership.

Which of the following is an appropriately-punctuated correction for this sentence?

a. Protestors filled the streets of the city, because they were dissatisfied with the government's leadership.

b. Protesters, filled the streets of the city, because they were dissatisfied with the government's leadership.

c. Because they were dissatisfied with the government's leadership protestors filled the streets of the city.

d. Protestors filled the streets of the city because they were dissatisfied with the government's leadership.

6. What is the part of speech of the underlined word in the sentence?

> We need to come up with a fresh <u>approach</u> to this problem.

a. Noun
b. Verb
c. Adverb
d. Adjective

7. What is the part of speech of the underlined word in the sentence?

> Investigators conducted an <u>exhaustive</u> inquiry into the accusations of corruption.

a. Noun
b. Verb
c. Adverb
d. Adjective

8. The underlined portion of the sentence is an example of which sentence component?

> New students should report <u>to the student center</u>.

a. Dependent clause
b. Adverbial phrase
c. Adjective clause
d. Noun phrase

9. What is the noun phrase in the following sentence?

> Charlotte's new German shepherd puppy is energetic.

a. Puppy
b. Charlotte
c. German shepherd puppy
d. Charlotte's new German shepherd puppy

10. Which word choices will correctly complete the sentence?

Increasing the price of bus fares has had a greater [affect / effect] on ridership [then / than] expected.

a. affect; then
b. affect; than
c. effect; then
d. effect; than

11. While studying vocabulary, a student notices that the words *circumference, circumnavigate,* and *circumstance* all begin with the prefix *circum–.* The student uses her knowledge of affixes to infer that all of these words share what related meaning?

a. Around, surrounding
b. Travel, transport
c. Size, measurement
d. Area, location

Reading Comprehension

Questions 1 – 6 are based on the following passage from The Curious Case of Benjamin Button *by F.S. Fitzgerald, 1922*

As long ago as 1860 it was the proper thing to be born at home. At present, so I am told, the high gods of medicine have decreed that the first cries of the young shall be uttered upon the anesthetic air of a hospital, preferably a fashionable one. So young Mr. and Mrs. Roger Button were fifty years ahead of style when they decided, one day in the summer of 1860, that their first baby should be born in a hospital. Whether this anachronism had any bearing upon the astonishing history I am about to set down will never be known.

I shall tell you what occurred, and let you judge for yourself.

The Roger Buttons held an enviable position, both social and financial, in ante-bellum Baltimore. They were related to the This Family and the That Family, which, as every Southerner knew, entitled them to membership in that enormous peerage which largely populated the Confederacy. This was their first experience with the charming old custom of having babies— Mr. Button was naturally nervous. He hoped it would be a boy so that he could be sent to Yale College in Connecticut, at which institution Mr. Button himself had been known for four years by the somewhat obvious nickname of "Cuff."

On the September morning <u>consecrated</u> to the enormous event he arose nervously at six o'clock dressed himself, adjusted an impeccable stock, and hurried forth through the streets of Baltimore to the hospital, to determine whether the darkness of the night had borne in new life upon its bosom.

When he was approximately a hundred yards from the Maryland Private Hospital for Ladies and Gentlemen he saw Doctor Keene, the family physician, descending the front steps, rubbing his hands together with a washing movement—as all doctors are required to do by the unwritten ethics of their profession.

Mr. Roger Button, the president of Roger Button & Co., Wholesale Hardware, began to run toward Doctor Keene with much less dignity than was expected from a Southern gentleman of that picturesque period. "Doctor Keene!" he called. "Oh, Doctor Keene!"

The doctor heard him, faced around, and stood waiting, a curious expression settling on his harsh, medicinal face as Mr. Button drew near.

"What happened?" demanded Mr. Button, as he came up in a gasping rush. "What was it? How is she? A boy? Who is it? What—"

"Talk sense!" said Doctor Keene sharply. He appeared somewhat irritated.

"Is the child born?" begged Mr. Button.

Doctor Keene frowned. "Why, yes, I suppose so—after a fashion." Again he threw a curious glance at Mr. Button.

1. What major event is about to happen in this story?
   a. Mr. Button is about to go to a funeral.
   b. Mr. Button's wife is about to have a baby.
   c. Mr. Button is getting ready to go to the doctor's office.
   d. Mr. Button is about to go shopping for new clothes.

2. What kind of tone does the above passage have?
   a. Nervous and Excited
   b. Sad and Angry
   c. Shameful and Confused
   d. Grateful and Joyous

3. What is the meaning of the word "consecrated" in paragraph 4?
   a. Numbed
   b. Chained
   c. Dedicated
   d. Moved

4. What does the author mean to do by adding the following statement?

   "rubbing his hands together with a washing movement—as all doctors are required to do by the unwritten ethics of their profession."

   a. Suggesting that Mr. Button is tired of the doctor.
   b. Trying to explain the detail of the doctor's profession.
   c. Hinting to readers that the doctor is an unethical man.
   d. Giving readers a visual picture of what the doctor is doing.

5. Which of the following best describes the development of this passage?
   a. It starts in the middle of a narrative in order to transition smoothly to a conclusion.
   b. It is a chronological narrative from beginning to end.
   c. The sequence of events is backwards—we go from future events to past events.
   d. To introduce the setting of the story and its characters.

6. Which of the following is an example of an imperative sentence?
   a. "Oh, Doctor Keene!"
   b. "Talk sense!"
   c. "Is the child born?"
   d. "Why, yes, I suppose so—"

Questions 7–12 are based on the following excerpt from "The Story of An Hour" by Kate Chopin

Knowing that Mrs. Mallard was afflicted with heart trouble, great care was taken to break to her as gently as possible the news of her husband's death.

It was her sister Josephine who told her, in broken sentences; veiled hints that revealed in half concealing. Her husband's friend Richards was there, too, near her. It was he who had been in the newspaper office when intelligence of the railroad disaster was received, with Brently Mallard's name leading the list of "killed." He had only taken the time to assure himself of its truth by a second telegram, and had hastened to forestall any less careful, less tender friend in bearing the sad message.

She did not hear the story as many women have heard the same, with a paralyzed inability to accept its significance. She wept at once, with sudden, wild abandonment, in her sister's arms. When the storm of grief had spent itself she went away to her room alone. She would have no one follow her.

There stood, facing the open window, a comfortable, roomy armchair. Into this she sank, pressed down by a physical exhaustion that haunted her body and seemed to reach into her soul.

She could see in the open square before her house the tops of trees that were all aquiver with the new spring life. The delicious breath of rain was in the air. In the street below a peddler was crying his wares. The notes of a distant song which some one was singing reached her faintly, and countless sparrows were twittering in the eaves.

There were patches of blue sky showing here and there through the clouds that had met and piled one above the other in the west facing her window.

She sat with her head thrown back upon the cushion of the chair, quite motionless, except when a sob came up into her throat and shook her, as a child who has cried itself to sleep continues to sob in its dreams.

She was young, with a fair, calm face, whose lines bespoke repression and even a certain strength. But now here was a dull stare in her eyes, whose gaze was fixed away off yonder on one of those patches of blue sky. It was not a glance of reflection, but rather indicated a suspension of intelligent thought.

There was something coming to her and she was waiting for it, fearfully. What was it? She did not know; it was too subtle and elusive to name. But she felt it, creeping out of the sky, reaching toward her through the sounds, the scents, and color that filled the air.

Now her bosom rose and fell tumultuously. She was beginning to recognize this thing that was approaching to possess her, and she was striving to beat it back with her will—as powerless as her two white slender hands would have been. When she abandoned herself a little whispered word escaped her slightly parted lips. She said it over and over under her breath: "free, free, free!" The vacant stare and the look of terror that had followed it went from her eyes. They stayed keen and bright. Her pulses beat fast, and the coursing blood warmed and relaxed every inch of her body.

She did not stop to ask if it were or were not a monstrous joy that held her. A clear and exalted perception enabled her to dismiss the suggestion as trivial. She knew that she would weep again when she saw the kind, tender hands folded in death; the face that had never looked save with love upon her, fixed and gray and dead. But she saw beyond that bitter moment a long procession of years to come that would belong to her absolutely. And she opened and spread her arms out to them in welcome.

7. What point of view is the above passage told in?
   a. First person
   b. Second person
   c. Third person omniscient
   d. Third person limited

8. What kind of irony are we presented with in this story?
   a. The way Mrs. Mallard reacted to her husband's death.
   b. The way in which Mr. Mallard died.
   c. The way in which the news of her husband's death was presented to Mrs. Mallard.
   d. The way in which nature is compared with death in the story.

9. What is the meaning of the word "elusive" in paragraph 9?
   a. Horrible
   b. Indefinable
   c. Quiet
   d. Joyful

10. What is the best summary of the passage above?
    a. Mr. Mallard, a soldier during World War I, is killed by the enemy and leaves his wife widowed.
    b. Mrs. Mallard understands the value of friendship when her friends show up for her after her husband's death.
    c. Mrs. Mallard combats mental illness daily and will perhaps be sent to a mental institution soon.
    d. Mrs. Mallard, a newly widowed woman, finds unexpected relief in her husband's death.

11. What is the tone of this story?
    a. Confused
    b. Joyful
    c. Depressive
    d. All of the above

12. What is the meaning of the word "tumultuously" in paragraph 10?
    a. Orderly
    b. Unashamedly
    c. Violently
    d. Calmly

The poem below, "The Human Seasons," was written by John Keats. Read it and answer questions 13 –
19.

> Four Seasons fill the measure of the year;
> There are four seasons in the mind of man:
> He has his lusty Spring, when fancy clear
> Takes in all beauty with an easy span:
> 5   He has his Summer, when luxuriously
> Spring's honied cud of youthful thought he loves
> To ruminate, and by such dreaming high
> Is nearest unto heaven: quiet coves
> His soul has in its Autumn, when his wings
> 10   He furleth close; contented so to look
> On mists in idleness—to let fair things
> Pass by unheeded as a threshold brook.
> He has his Winter too of pale misfeature,
> Or else he would forego his mortal nature.

13. What literary device does Keats primarily use in this poem?
    a. Simile
    b. Soliloquy
    c. Hyperbole
    d. Extended metaphor

14. The meaning of the word "ruminate" in line 7 is closest to:
    a. Ponder
    b. Unwind
    c. Respond
    d. Incorporate

15. According to the poem, how does a man change between Spring and Autumn?
    a. He starts preparing for his future.
    b. He feels more deeply connected to nature.
    c. He spends less time thinking about beautiful things.
    d. He becomes more sensible about how he spends his time.

16. Why does Keats end the poem with Winter?
    a. Winter represents the end of man's life.
    b. The narrator's least favorite season is winter.
    c. Winter is the final season of the calendar year.
    d. The poem is organized from the hottest season to the coldest.

17. Which statement would the narrator probably agree with?
    a. People are most content when they are young.
    b. People should appreciate the beauty of everyday life more.
    c. People change as they move through different stages of life.
    d. People spend too much time on daydreaming instead of being active.

18. What does "he would forego his mortal nature" mean in the final line?
    a. He would take a break.
    b. He would postpone or avoid death.
    c. He would give up nature for technology.
    d. He would move away from the countryside.

19. Which of the following is an example of alliteration in this poem?
    a. "in the mind of man"
    b. "On mists of idleness"
    c. "his wings / He furleth closed"
    d. "unheeded as a threshold brook"

Read this article about NASA technology and answer questions 20–25.

When researchers and engineers undertake a large-scale scientific project, they may end up making discoveries and developing technologies that have far wider uses than originally intended. This is especially true in NASA, one of the most influential and innovative scientific organizations in America. NASA *spinoff technology* refers to innovations originally developed for NASA space projects that are now used in a wide range of different commercial fields. Many consumers are unaware that products they are buying are based on NASA research! Spinoff technology proves that it's worthwhile to invest in science research because it could enrich people's lives in unexpected ways.

The first spinoff technology worth mentioning is baby food. In space, where astronauts have limited access to fresh food and fewer options about their daily meals, malnutrition is a serious concern. Consequently, NASA researchers were looking for ways to enhance the nutritional value of astronauts' food. Scientists found that a certain type of algae could be added to food, improving the food's neurological benefits. When experts in the commercial food industry learned of this algae's potential to boost brain health, they were quick to begin their own research. The nutritional substance from algae then developed into a product called life's DHA, which can be found in over 90 percent of infant food sold in America.

Another intriguing example of a spinoff technology can be found in fashion. People who are always dropping their sunglasses may have invested in a pair of sunglasses with scratch resistant lenses—that is, it's impossible to scratch the glass, even if the glasses are dropped on an abrasive surface. This innovation is incredibly advantageous for people who are clumsy, but most shoppers don't know that this technology was originally developed by NASA. Scientists first created scratch resistant glass to help protect costly and crucial equipment from getting scratched in space, especially the helmet visors in space suits. However, sunglasses companies later realized that this technology could be profitable for their products, and they licensed the technology from NASA.

20. What is the main purpose of this article?
    a. To advise consumers to do more research before making a purchase
    b. To persuade readers to support NASA research
    c. To tell a narrative about the history of space technology
    d. To define and describe examples of spinoff technology

21. What is the organizational structure of this article?
    a. A general definition followed by more specific examples
    b. A general opinion followed by supporting arguments
    c. An important moment in history followed by chronological details
    d. A popular misconception followed by counterevidence

22. Why did NASA scientists research algae?
    a. They already knew algae was healthy for babies.
    b. They were interested in how to grow food in space.
    c. They were looking for ways to add health benefits to food.
    d. They hoped to use it to protect expensive research equipment.

23. What does the word "neurological" mean in the second paragraph?
    a. Related to the body
    b. Related to the brain
    c. Related to vitamins
    d. Related to technology

24. Why does the author mention space suit helmets?
    a. To give an example of astronaut fashion
    b. To explain where sunglasses got their shape
    c. To explain how astronauts protect their eyes
    d. To give an example of valuable space equipment

25. Which statement would the author probably NOT agree with?
    a. Consumers don't always know the history of the products they are buying.
    b. Sometimes new innovations have unexpected applications.
    c. It's difficult to make money from scientific research.
    d. Space equipment is often very expensive.

Questions 26–29 are based on the following passage:

Smoking tobacco products is terribly destructive. A single cigarette contains over 4,000 chemicals, including 43 known carcinogens and 400 deadly toxins. Some of the most dangerous ingredients include tar, carbon monoxide, formaldehyde, ammonia, arsenic, and DDT. Smoking can cause numerous types of cancer including throat, mouth, nasal cavity, esophagus, stomach, pancreas, kidney, bladder, and cervical.

Cigarettes contain a drug called nicotine, one of the most addictive substances known to man. Addiction is defined as a compulsion to seek the substance despite negative consequences. According to the National Institute of Drug Abuse, nearly 35 million smokers expressed a desire to quit smoking in 2015; however, more than 85 percent of those addicts will not achieve their goal. Almost all smokers regret picking up that first cigarette. You would be wise to learn from their mistake if you have not yet started smoking.

According to the U.S. Department of Health and Human Services, 16 million people in the United States presently suffer from a smoking-related condition and nearly nine million suffer from a serious smoking-related illness. According to the Centers for Disease Control and Prevention (CDC), tobacco products cause nearly six million deaths per year. This number is projected to rise to over eight million deaths by 2030. Smokers, on average, die ten years earlier than their nonsmoking peers.

In the United States, local, state, and federal governments typically tax tobacco products, which leads to high prices. Nicotine addicts sometimes pay more for a pack of cigarettes than for a few gallons of gas. Additionally, smokers tend to stink. The smell of smoke is all-consuming and creates a pervasive nastiness. Smokers also risk staining their teeth and fingers with yellow residue from the tar.

Smoking is deadly, expensive, and socially unappealing. Clearly, smoking is not worth the risks.

26. Which of the following best describes the passage?
    a. Narrative
    b. Persuasive
    c. Expository
    d. Technical

27. Which of the following statements most accurately summarizes the passage?
    a. Tobacco is less healthy than many alternatives.
    b. Tobacco is deadly, expensive, and socially unappealing, and smokers would be much better off kicking the addiction.
    c. In the United States, local, state, and federal governments typically tax tobacco products, which leads to high prices.
    d. Tobacco products shorten smokers' lives by ten years and kill more than six million people per year.

28. The author would be most likely to agree with which of the following statements?
    a. Smokers should only quit cold turkey and avoid all nicotine cessation devices.
    b. Other substances are more addictive than tobacco.
    c. Smokers should quit for whatever reason that gets them to stop smoking.
    d. People who want to continue smoking should advocate for a reduction in tobacco product taxes.

29. Which of the following represents an opinion statement on the part of the author?
    a. According to the Centers for Disease Control and Prevention (CDC), tobacco products cause nearly six million deaths per year.
    b. Nicotine addicts sometimes pay more for a pack of cigarettes than a few gallons of gas.
    c. They also risk staining their teeth and fingers with yellow residue from the tar.
    d. Additionally, smokers tend to stink. The smell of smoke is all-consuming and creates a pervasive nastiness.

Questions 30–34 are based on the following passage:

Christopher Columbus is often credited for discovering America. This is incorrect. First, it is impossible to "discover" somewhere where people already live; however, Christopher Columbus did explore places in the New World that were previously untouched by Europe, so the term "explorer" would be more accurate. Another correction must be made, as well: Christopher Columbus was not the first European explorer to reach the present-day Americas! Rather, it was Leif Erikson who first came to the New World and contacted the natives, nearly five hundred years before Christopher Columbus.

Leif Erikson, the son of Erik the Red (a famous Viking outlaw and explorer in his own right), was born in either 970 or 980, depending on which historian you seek. His own family, though, did not raise Leif, which was a Viking tradition. Instead, one of Erik's prisoners taught Leif reading and writing, languages, sailing, and weaponry. At age 12, Leif was considered a man and returned to his family. He killed a man during a dispute shortly after his return, and the council banished the Erikson clan to Greenland.

In 999, Leif left Greenland and traveled to Norway where he would serve as a guard to King Olaf Tryggvason. It was there that he became a convert to Christianity. Leif later tried to return home with the intention of taking supplies and spreading Christianity to Greenland, however his ship was blown off course and he arrived in a strange new land: present day Newfoundland, Canada.

When he finally returned to his adopted homeland Greenland, Leif consulted with a merchant who had also seen the shores of this previously unknown land we now know as Canada. The son of the legendary Viking explorer then gathered a crew of 35 men and set sail. Leif became the first European to touch foot in the New World as he explored present-day Baffin Island and Labrador, Canada. His crew called the land "Vinland," since it was plentiful with grapes.

During their time in present-day Newfoundland, Leif's expedition made contact with the natives whom they referred to as Skraelings (which translates to "wretched ones" in Norse). There are several secondhand accounts of their meetings. Some contemporaries described trade between the peoples. Other accounts describe clashes where the Skraelings defeated the Viking explorers with long spears, while still others claim the Vikings dominated the natives. Regardless of the circumstances, it seems that the Vikings made contact of some kind. This happened around 1000, nearly five hundred years before Columbus famously sailed the ocean blue.

Eventually, in 1003, Leif set sail for home and arrived at Greenland with a ship full of timber. In 1020, seventeen years later, the legendary Viking died. Many believe that Leif Erikson should receive more credit for his contributions in exploring the New World.

30. Which of the following best describes how the author generally presents the information?
    a. Chronological order
    b. Comparison-contrast
    c. Cause-effect
    d. Conclusion-premises

31. Which of the following is an opinion, rather than historical fact, expressed by the author?
    a. Leif Erikson was definitely the son of Erik the Red; however, historians debate the year of his birth.
    b. Leif Erikson's crew called the land "Vinland," since it was plentiful with grapes.
    c. Leif Erikson deserves more credit for his contributions in exploring the New World.
    d. Leif Erikson explored the Americas nearly five hundred years before Christopher Columbus.

32. Which of the following most accurately describes the author's main conclusion?
    a. Leif Erikson is a legendary Viking explorer.
    b. Leif Erikson deserves more credit for exploring America hundreds of years before Columbus.
    c. Spreading Christianity motivated Leif Erikson's expeditions more than any other factor.
    d. Leif Erikson contacted the natives nearly five hundred years before Columbus.

33. Which of the following best describes the author's intent in the passage?
    a. To entertain
    b. To inform
    c. To alert
    d. To suggest

34. Which of the following can be logically inferred from the passage?
    a. The Vikings disliked exploring the New World.
    b. Leif Erikson's banishment from Iceland led to his exploration of present-day Canada.
    c. Leif Erikson never shared his stories of exploration with the King of Norway.
    d. Historians have difficulty definitively pinpointing events in the Vikings' history.

Questions 20-27 are based on the following passages:

Passage I

Lethal force, or deadly force, is defined as the physical means to cause death or serious harm to another individual. The law holds that lethal force is only accepted when you or another person are in immediate and unavoidable danger of death or severe bodily harm. For example, a person could be beating a weaker person in such a way that they are suffering severe enough trauma that could result in death or serious harm. This would be an instance where lethal force would be acceptable and possibly the only way to save that person from irrevocable damage.

Another example of when to use lethal force would be when someone enters your home with a deadly weapon. The intruder's presence and possession of the weapon indicate mal-intent and the ability to inflict death or severe injury to you and your loved ones. Again, lethal force can be used in this situation. Lethal force can also be applied to prevent the harm of another individual. If a woman is being brutally assaulted and is unable to fend off an attacker, lethal force can be used to defend her as a last-ditch effort. If she is in immediate jeopardy of rape, harm, and/or death, lethal force could be the only response that could effectively deter the assailant.

The key to understanding the concept of lethal force is the term *last resort*. Deadly force cannot be taken back; it should be used only to prevent severe harm or death. The law does distinguish whether the means of one's self-defense is fully warranted, or if the individual goes out of control in the process. If you continually attack the assailant after they are rendered incapacitated, this would be causing unnecessary harm, and the law can bring charges against you. Likewise, if you kill an attacker unnecessarily after defending yourself, you can be charged with murder. This would move lethal force beyond necessary defense, making it no longer a last resort but rather a use of excessive force.

Passage II

Assault is the unlawful attempt of one person to apply apprehension on another individual by an imminent threat or by initiating offensive contact. Assaults can vary, encompassing physical strikes, threatening body language, and even provocative language. In the case of the latter, even if a hand has not been laid, it is still considered an assault because of its threatening nature.

Let's look at an example: A homeowner is angered because his neighbor blows fallen leaves into his freshly mowed lawn. Irate, the homeowner gestures a fist to his fellow neighbor and threatens to bash his head in for littering on his lawn. The homeowner's physical motions and verbal threat heralds a physical threat against the other neighbor. These factors classify the homeowner's reaction as an assault. If the angry neighbor hits the threatening homeowner in retaliation, that would constitute an assault as well because he physically hit the homeowner.

Assault also centers on the involvement of weapons in a conflict. If someone fires a gun at another person, this could be interpreted as an assault unless the shooter acted in self-defense. If an individual drew a gun or a knife on someone with the intent to harm them, that would be considered assault. However, it's also considered an assault if someone simply aimed a weapon, loaded or not, at another person in a threatening manner.

35. What is the purpose of the second passage?
    a. To inform the reader about what assault is and how it is committed
    b. To inform the reader about how assault is a minor example of lethal force
    c. To disprove the previous passage concerning lethal force
    d. The author is recounting an incident in which they were assaulted

36. Which of the following situations, according to the passages, would not constitute an illegal use of lethal force?
    a. A disgruntled cash register yells obscenities at a customer.
    b. A thief is seen running away with stolen cash.
    c. A man is attacked in an alley by another man with a knife.
    d. A woman punches another woman in a bar.

37. Given the information in the passages, which of the following must be true about assault?
    a. Assault charges are more severe than unnecessary use of force charges.
    b. There are various forms of assault.
    c. Smaller, weaker people cannot commit assaults.
    d. Assault is justified only as a last resort.

38. Which of the following, if true, would most seriously undermine the explanation proposed by the author in Passage I in the third paragraph?

    a. An instance of lethal force in self-defense is not absolutely absolved from blame. The law considers the necessary use of force at the time it is committed.

    b. An individual who uses lethal force under necessary defense is in direct compliance of the law under most circumstances.

    c. Lethal force in self-defense should be forgiven in all cases for the peace of mind of the primary victim.

    d. The use of lethal force is not evaluated on the intent of the user, but rather the severity of the primary attack that warranted self-defense.

39. Based on the passages, what can be inferred about the relationship between assault and lethal force?

    a. An act of lethal force always leads to a type of assault.

    b. An assault will result in someone using lethal force.

    c. An assault with deadly intent can lead to an individual using lethal force to preserve their well-being.

    d. If someone uses self-defense in a conflict, it is called deadly force; if actions or threats are intended, it is called assault.

40. Which of the following best describes the way the passages are structured?

    a. Both passages open by defining a legal concept and then continue to describe situations that further explain the concept.

    b. Both passages begin with situations, introduce accepted definitions, and then cite legal ramifications.

    c. Passage I presents a long definition while the Passage II begins by showing an example of assault.

    d. Both cite specific legal doctrines, then proceed to explain the rulings.

Questions 41–45 are based on the following passage:

In the quest to understand existence, modern philosophers must question if humans can fully comprehend the world. Classical western approaches to philosophy tend to hold that one can understand something, be it an event or object, by standing outside of the phenomena and observing it. It is then by unbiased observation that one can grasp the details of the world. This seems to hold true for many things. Scientists conduct experiments and record their findings, and thus many natural phenomena become comprehendible. However, several of these observations were possible because humans used tools in order to make these discoveries.

This may seem like an extraneous matter. After all, people invented things like microscopes and telescopes in order to enhance their capacity to view cells or the movement of stars. While humans are still capable of seeing things, the question remains if human beings have the capacity to fully observe and see the world in order to understand it. It would not be an impossible stretch to argue that what humans see through a microscope is not the exact thing itself, but a human interpretation of it.

This would seem to be the case in the "Business of the Holes" experiment conducted by Richard Feynman. To study the way electrons behave, Feynman set up a barrier with two holes and a plate. The plate was there to indicate how many times the electrons would pass through the hole(s). Rather than casually observe the electrons acting under normal circumstances, Feynman discovered that electrons behave in two totally different ways depending on whether or not they are observed. The electrons that were observed had passed through either one of the holes or were caught on the plate as particles. However, electrons that weren't observed acted as waves instead of particles and passed through both holes. This indicated that electrons have a dual nature. Electrons seen by the human eye act like particles, while unseen electrons act like waves of energy.

This dual nature of the electrons presents a conundrum. While humans now have a better understanding of electrons, the fact remains that people cannot entirely perceive how electrons behave without the use of instruments. We can only observe one of the mentioned behaviors, which only provides a partial understanding of the entire function of electrons. Therefore, we're forced to ask ourselves whether the world we observe is objective or if it is subjectively perceived by humans. Or, an alternative question: can man understand the world only through machines that will allow them to observe natural phenomena?

Both questions humble man's capacity to grasp the world. However, those ideas don't consider that many phenomena have been proven by human beings without the use of machines, such as the discovery of gravity. Like all philosophical questions, whether man's reason and observation alone can understand the universe can be approached from many angles.

41. The word *extraneous* in paragraph two can be best interpreted as referring to which one of the following?
   a. Indispensable
   b. Bewildering
   c. Superfluous
   d. Exuberant

42. What is the author's motivation for writing the passage?
   a. To bring to light an alternative view on human perception by examining the role of technology in human understanding.
   b. To educate the reader on the latest astroparticle physics discovery and offer terms that may be unfamiliar to the reader.
   c. To argue that humans are totally blind to the realities of the world by presenting an experiment that proves that electrons are not what they seem on the surface.
   d. To reflect on opposing views of human understanding.

43. Which of the following most closely resembles the way in which paragraph four is structured?
   a. It offers one solution, questions the solution, and then ends with an alternative solution.
   b. It presents an inquiry, explains the details of that inquiry, and then offers a solution.
   c. It presents a problem, explains the details of that problem, and then ends with more inquiry.
   d. It gives a definition, offers an explanation, and then ends with an inquiry.

44. For the classical approach to understanding to hold true, which of the following must be required?
    a. A telescope
    b. A recording device
    c. Multiple witnesses present
    d. The person observing must be unbiased

45. Which best describes how the electrons in the experiment behaved like waves?
    a. The electrons moved up and down like actual waves.
    b. The electrons passed through both holes and then onto the plate.
    c. The electrons converted to photons upon touching the plate.
    d. Electrons were seen passing through one hole or the other.

46. The author mentions "gravity" in the last paragraph in order to do what?
    a. In order to show that different natural phenomena test man's ability to grasp the world.
    b. To prove that since man has not measured it with the use of tools or machines, humans cannot know the true nature of gravity.
    c. To demonstrate an example of natural phenomena humans discovered and understand without the use of tools or machines.
    d. To show an alternative solution to the nature of electrons that humans have not thought of yet.

Answer Explanations

Editing/Revising

1. C: A complex sentence joins an independent or main clause with a dependent or subordinate clause. In this case, the main clause is "The restaurant is unconventional." This is a clause with one subject-verb combination that can stand alone as a grammatically-complete sentence. The dependent clause is "because it serves both Chicago style pizza and New York style pizza." This clause begins with the subordinating conjunction *because* and also consists of only one subject-verb combination. *A* is incorrect because a simple sentence consists of only one verb-subject combination—one independent clause. *B* is incorrect because a compound sentence contains two independent clauses connected by a conjunction. *D* is incorrect because a complex-compound sentence consists of two or more independent clauses and one or more dependent clauses.

2. A: Parallelism refers to consistent use of sentence structure or word form. In this case, the list within the sentence does not utilize parallelism; three of the verbs appear in their base form—*travel, take,* and *eat*—but one appears as a gerund—*going*. A parallel version of this sentence would be "This summer, I'm planning to travel to Italy, take a Mediterranean cruise, go to Pompeii, and eat a lot of Italian food." *B* is incorrect because this description is a complete sentence. *C* is incorrect as a misplaced modifier is a modifier that is not located appropriately in relation to the word or words they modify. *D* is incorrect because subject-verb agreement refers to the appropriate conjugation of a verb in relation to its subject.

3. C: In this sentence, the modifier is the phrase "Forgetting that he was supposed to meet his girlfriend for dinner." This phrase offers information about Fred's actions, but the noun that immediately follows it is Anita, creating some confusion about the "do-er" of the phrase. A more appropriate sentence arrangement would be "Forgetting that he was supposed to meet his girlfriend for dinner, Fred made Anita mad when he showed up late." *A* is incorrect as parallelism refers to the consistent use of sentence structure and verb tense, and this sentence is appropriately consistent. *B* is incorrect as a run-on sentence does not contain appropriate punctuation for the number of independent clauses presented, which is not true of this description. *D* is incorrect because subject-verb agreement refers to the appropriate conjugation of a verb relative to the subject, and all verbs have been properly conjugated.

4. B: A comma splice occurs when a comma is used to join two independent clauses together without the additional use of an appropriate conjunction. One way to remedy this problem is to replace the comma with a semicolon. Another solution is to add a conjunction: "Some workers use all their sick leave, but other workers cash out their leave." *A* is incorrect as parallelism refers to the consistent use of sentence structure and verb tense; all tenses and structures in this sentence are consistent. *C* is incorrect because a sentence fragment is a phrase or clause that cannot stand alone—this sentence contains two independent clauses. *D* is incorrect because subject-verb agreement refers to the proper conjugation of a verb relative to the subject, and all verbs have been properly conjugated.

5. D: The problem in the original passage is that the second sentence is a dependent clause that cannot stand alone as a sentence; it must be attached to the main clause found in the first sentence. Because the main clause comes first, it does not need to be separated by a comma. However, if the dependent clause came first, then a comma would be necessary, which is why Choice *C* is incorrect. *A* and *B* also insert unnecessary commas into the sentence.

6. A: A noun refers to a person, place, thing, or idea. Although the word *approach* can also be used as a verb, in the sentence it functions as a noun within the noun phrase "a fresh approach," so *B* is incorrect. An adverb is a word or phrase that provides additional information of the verb, but because the verb is *need* and not *approach*, then *C* is false. An adjective is a word that describes a noun, used here as the word *fresh*, but it is not the noun itself. Thus, *D* is also incorrect.

7. D: An adjective modifies a noun, answering the question "Which one?" or "What kind?" In this sentence, the word *exhaustive* is an adjective that modifies the noun *investigation*. Another clue that this word is an adjective is the suffix *–ive*, which means "having the quality of." The noun in this sentence is *investigators*; therefore, *A* is incorrect. The verb in this sentence is *conducted* because this was the action taken by the subject *the investigators*; therefore, *B* is incorrect. *C* is incorrect because an adverb is a word or phrase that provides additional information about the verb, expressing how, when, where, or in what manner.

8. B: In this case, the phrase functions as an adverb modifying the verb *report*, so *B* is the correct answer. "To the student center" does not consist of a subject-verb combination, so it is not a clause; thus, Choices *A* and *C* can be eliminated. This group of words is a phrase. Phrases are classified by either the controlling word in the phrase or its function in the sentence. *D* is incorrect because a noun phrase is a series of words that describe or modify a noun.

9. D: A noun phrase consists of the noun and all of its modifiers. In this case, the subject of the sentence is the noun *puppy*, but it is preceded by several modifiers—adjectives that give more information about what kind of puppy, which are also part of the noun phrase. Thus, *A* is incorrect. Charlotte is the owner of the puppy and a modifier of the puppy, so *B* is false. *C* is incorrect because it contains some, but not all, of the modifiers pertaining to the puppy. *D* is correct because it contains all of them.

10. D: In this sentence, the first answer choice requires a noun meaning *impact* or *influence*, so *effect* is the correct answer. For the second answer choice, the sentence is drawing a comparison. *Than* shows a comparative relationship whereas *then* shows sequence or consequence. *A* and *C* can be eliminated because they contain the choice *then*. *B* is incorrect because *affect* is a verb while this sentence requires a noun.

11. A: The affix *circum–* originates from Latin and means *around or surrounding*. It is also related to other round words, such as circle and circus. The rest of the choices do not relate to the affix *circum–* and are therefore incorrect.

Reading Comprehension

1. B: Mr. Button's wife is about to have a baby. The passage begins by giving the reader information about traditional birthing situations. Then, we are told that Mr. and Mrs. Button decide to go against tradition to have their baby in a hospital. The next few passages are dedicated to letting the reader know how Mr. Button dresses and goes to the hospital to welcome his new baby. There is a doctor in this excerpt, as Choice *C* indicates, and Mr. Button does put on clothes, as Choice *D* indicates. However, Mr. Button is not going to the doctor's office nor is he about to go shopping for new clothes.

2. A: The tone of the above passage is nervous and excited. We are told in the fourth paragraph that Mr. Button "arose nervously." We also see him running without caution to the doctor to find out about his wife and baby—this indicates his excitement. We also see him stuttering in a nervous yet excited fashion as he asks the doctor if it's a boy or girl. Though the doctor may seem a bit abrupt at the end, indicating a bit of anger or shame, neither of these choices is the overwhelming tone of the entire passage.

3. C: Dedicated. Mr. Button is dedicated to the task before him. Choice A, numbed, Choice B, chained, and Choice D, moved, all could grammatically fit in the sentence. However, they are not synonyms with *consecrated* like Choice C is.

4. D: Giving readers a visual picture of what the doctor is doing. The author describes a visual image—the doctor rubbing his hands together—first and foremost. The author may be trying to make a comment about the profession; however, the author does not "explain the detail of the doctor's profession" as Choice B suggests.

5. D: To introduce the setting of the story and its characters. We know we are being introduced to the setting because we are given the year in the very first paragraph along with the season: "one day in the summer of 1860." This is a classic structure of an introduction of the setting. We are also getting a long explanation of Mr. Button, what his work is, who is related to him, and what his life is like in the third paragraph.

6. B: "Talk sense!" is an example of an imperative sentence. An imperative sentence gives a command. The doctor is commanding Mr. Button to talk sense. Choice A is an example of an exclamatory sentence, which expresses excitement. Choice C is an example of an interrogative sentence—these types of sentences ask questions. Choice D is an example of a declarative sentence. This means that the character is simply making a statement.

7. C: The point of view is told in third person omniscient. We know this because the story starts out with us knowing something that the character does not know: that her husband has died. Mrs. Mallard eventually comes to know this, but we as readers know this information before it is broken to her. In third person limited, Choice D, we would only see and know what Mrs. Mallard herself knew, and we would find out the news of her husband's death when she found out the news, not before.

8. A: The way Mrs. Mallard reacted to her husband's death. The irony in this story is called situational irony, which means the situation that takes place is different than what the audience anticipated. At the beginning of the story, we see Mrs. Mallard react with a burst of grief to her husband's death. However, once she's alone, she begins to contemplate her future and says the word "free" over and over. This is quite a different reaction from Mrs. Mallard than what readers expected from the first of the story.

9. B: The word "elusive" most closely means "indefinable." Horrible, Choice A, doesn't quite fit with the tone of the word "subtle" that comes before it. Choice C, "quiet," is more closely related to the word "subtle." Choice D, "joyful," also doesn't quite fit the context here. "Indefinable" is the best option.

10. D: Mrs. Mallard, a newly widowed woman, finds unexpected relief in her husband's death. A summary is a brief explanation of the main point of a story. The story mostly focuses on Mrs. Mallard and her reaction to her husband's death, especially in the room when she's alone and contemplating the present and future. All of the other answer choices except Choice C are briefly mentioned in the story; however, they are not the main focus of the story.

11. D: The interesting thing about this story is that feelings that are confused, joyful, and depressive all play a unique and almost equal part of this story. There is no one right answer here, because the author seems to display all of these emotions through the character of Mrs. Mallard. She displays feelings of depressiveness by her grief at the beginning; then, when she receives feelings of joy, she feels moments of confusion. We as readers cannot help but go through these feelings with the character. Thus, the author creates a tone of depression, joy, and confusion, all in one story.

12. C: The word "tumultuously" most nearly means "violently." Even if you don't know the word "tumultuously," look at the surrounding context to figure it out. The next few sentences we see Mrs. Mallard striving to "beat back" the "thing that was approaching to possess her." We see a fearful and almost violent reaction to the emotion that she's having. Thus, her chest would rise and fall turbulently, or violently.

13. D: Extended metaphor. Metaphor is a direct comparison between two things, and extended metaphor is a lengthy, well-developed metaphor that usually extends over the length of the poem. In this poem, Keats forms an extended metaphor by drawing a comparison between the four seasons of nature and the "seasons" that humans experience from youth to old age.

14. A: Ponder. This question can be answered using context clues from the sentence: "Spring's honied cud of youthful thought he loves / To ruminate, and by such dreaming high / Is nearest unto heaven." Following the word "ruminate," it's restated as "such dreaming"; also, immediately before is the expression "youthful thought." Together, this sentence describes a young man pleasantly daydreaming. The only word related to thinking and daydreaming is "ponder," Choice *A*.

15. C: He spends less time thinking about beautiful things. This is a general comprehension question. The narrator describes a man in Autumn "contented so . . . to let fair things / Pass by unheeded." In this case, "fair" is another word for "beautiful," and letting things "pass by unheeded" means "he doesn't pay attention to them." In contrast, a man in the Spring and Summer of life spends time appreciating and daydreaming about beautiful things.

16. A: Winter represents the end of man's life. This is a purpose question, but it also requires readers to understand that this poem is an extended metaphor. Since the narrator is developing an extended comparison between seasons and life, it's natural that winter should come last because it's the season of death, dormancy, and "pale" nature (unlike, say, Spring, which is a season of life and rebirth in nature).

17. C: People change as they move through different stages of life. This is an inference question asking readers to understand the narrator's perspective. Choices *B* and *D* both include an opinion or advice to the reader, while the tone of the poem is more neutral or purely descriptive (the narrator is simply describing the stages of life, rather than advising readers on how to behave). Choice *C* more closely agrees with the comparison that the narrator sets up in the poem; just as seasons change in nature, people also change throughout their lives.

18. B: He would postpone or avoid death. This is both a vocabulary and a comprehension question. Based on the poem's extended metaphor, readers can gather that Winter is a metaphor for the end of life; all people must pass through Winter or else they would never die. Looking at the poem's vocabulary, "mortal" refers to human's limited life span (the opposite of "immortal"), and "forego" means to turn something down.

19. A: "in the mind of man" (2). This is a fairly straightforward question about literary devices. Alliteration refers to repetition of a word's beginning sound, and Choice *A* is the only example of that ("mind" and "man" both start with the letter M).

20. D: To define and describe examples of spinoff technology. This is a purpose question—*why* did the author write this? The article contains facts, definitions, and other objective information without telling a story or arguing an opinion. In this case, the purpose of the article is to inform the reader. The only answer choice related to giving information is Choice *D*: to define and describe.

21. A: A general definition followed by more specific examples. This organization question asks readers to analyze the structure of the essay. The topic of the essay is spinoff technology; the first paragraph gives a general definition of the concept, while the following two paragraphs offer more detailed examples to help illustrate this idea.

22. C: They were looking for ways to add health benefits to food. This reading comprehension question can be answered based on the second paragraph—scientists were concerned about astronauts' nutrition and began researching nutritional supplements. Choice A isn't true because it reverses the order of discovery (first NASA identified algae for astronaut use, and then it was further developed for use in baby food).

23. B: Related to the brain. This vocabulary question could be answered based on the reader's prior knowledge, but the passage provides context clues for readers who've never encountered the word "neurological." The next sentence talks about "this algae's potential to boost brain health," which is a paraphrase of "neurological benefits." From this context, readers should be able to infer that "neurological" relates to the brain.

24. D: To give an example of valuable space equipment. This purpose question requires readers to understand the relevance of the given detail. In this case, the author mentions "costly and crucial equipment" before space suit visors, which are given as an example of something valuable. Choice A isn't correct because fashion is only related to sunglasses, not to NASA equipment. Choice B can be eliminated because it's simply not mentioned. While Choice C seems like it could be true, it's not relevant.

25. C: It's difficult to make money from scientific research. The article gives several examples of how businesses have capitalized on NASA research, so it's unlikely that the author would agree with this statement. Evidence for the other answer choices can be found in the article: In Choice A, the author mentions that "many consumers are unaware that products they are buying are based on NASA research"; Choice B is a general definition of spinoff technology; and Choice D is mentioned in the final paragraph.

26. B: Narrative, Choice A, means a written account of connected events. Think of narrative writing as a story. Choice C, expository writing, generally seeks to explain or describe some phenomena, whereas Choice D, technical writing, includes directions, instructions, and/or explanations. This passage is definitely persuasive writing, which hopes to change someone's beliefs based on an appeal to reason or emotion. The author is aiming to convince the reader that smoking is terrible. They use health, price, and beauty in their argument against smoking, so Choice B, persuasive, is the correct answer.

27. B: The author is clearly opposed to tobacco. He cites disease and deaths associated with smoking. He points to the monetary expense and aesthetic costs. Choice A is wrong because alternatives to smoking are not even addressed in the passage. Choice C is wrong because it does not summarize the passage; rather, it is just a premise. Choice D is wrong because, while these statistics do support the argument, they do not represent a summary of the piece. Choice C is the correct answer because it states the three critiques offered against tobacco and expresses the author's conclusion.

28. C: We are looking for something the author would agree with, so it will almost certainly be anti-smoking or an argument in favor of quitting smoking. Choice A is wrong because the author does not speak against means of cessation. Choice B is wrong because the author does not reference other substances, but does speak of how addictive nicotine—a drug in tobacco—is. Choice D is wrong because the author certainly would not encourage reducing taxes to encourage a reduction of smoking costs, thereby helping smokers to continue the habit. Choice *C* is correct because the author is definitely attempting to persuade smokers to quit smoking.

29. D: Here, we are looking for an opinion of the author's rather than a fact or statistic. Choice *A* is wrong because quoting statistics from the Centers of Disease Control and Prevention is stating facts, not opinions. Choice *B* is wrong because it expresses the fact that cigarettes sometimes cost more than a few gallons of gas. It would be an opinion if the author said that cigarettes were not affordable. Choice *C* is incorrect because yellow stains are a known possible adverse effect of smoking. Choice *D* is correct as an opinion because smell is subjective. Some people might like the smell of smoke, they might not have working olfactory senses, and/or some people might not find the smell of smoke akin to "pervasive nastiness," so this is the expression of an opinion. Thus, Choice *D* is the correct answer.

30. D: The passage does not proceed in chronological order since it begins by pointing out Leif Erikson's explorations in America, so Choice *A* does not work. Although the author compares and contrasts Erikson with Christopher Columbus, this is not the main way in which the information is presented; therefore, Choice *B* does not work. Neither does Choice *C* because there is no mention of or reference to cause and effect in the passage. However, the passage does offer a conclusion (Leif Erikson deserves more credit) and premises (first European to set foot in the New World and first to contact the natives) to substantiate Erikson's historical importance. Thus, Choice *D* is correct.

31. C: Choice *A* is wrong because it describes facts: Leif Erikson was the son of Erik the Red and historians debate Leif's date of birth. These are not opinions. Choice *B* is wrong; that Erikson called the land "Vinland" is a verifiable fact, as is Choice *D* because he did contact the natives almost 500 years before Columbus. Choice *C* is the correct answer because it is the author's opinion that Erikson deserves more credit. That, in fact, is his conclusion in the piece, but another person could argue that Columbus or another explorer deserves more credit for opening up the New World to exploration. Rather than being an indisputable fact, it is a subjective value claim.

32. B: Choice *A* is wrong because the author aims to go beyond describing Erikson as a mere legendary Viking. Choice *C* is wrong because the author does not focus on Erikson's motivations, let alone name the spreading of Christianity as his primary objective. Choice *D* is wrong because it is a premise that Erikson contacted the natives 500 years before Columbus, which is simply a part of supporting the author's conclusion. Choice *B* is correct because, as stated in the previous answer, it accurately identifies the author's statement that Erikson deserves more credit than he has received for being the first European to explore the New World.

33. B: Choice *A* is wrong because the author is not in any way trying to entertain the reader. Choice *D* is wrong because he goes beyond a mere suggestion; "suggest" is too vague. Although the author is certainly trying to alert the readers (make them aware) of Leif Erikson's underappreciated and unheralded accomplishments, the nature of the writing does not indicate the author would be satisfied with the reader merely knowing of Erikson's exploration (Choice *C*). Rather, the author would want the reader to be informed about it, which is more substantial (Choice *B*).

34. D: Choice *A* is wrong because the author never addresses the Vikings' state of mind or emotions. Choice *B* is wrong because the author does not elaborate on Erikson's exile and whether he would have become an explorer if not for his banishment. Choice *C* is wrong because there is not enough information to support this premise. It is unclear whether Erikson informed the King of Norway of his finding. Although it is true that the King did not send a follow-up expedition, he could have simply chosen not to expend the resources after receiving Erikson's news. It is not possible to logically infer whether Erikson told him. Choice *D* is correct because there are two examples—Leif Erikson's date of birth and what happened during the encounter with the natives—of historians having trouble pinning down important dates in Viking history.

35. A: The purpose is to inform the reader about what assault is and how it is committed. Choice *B* is incorrect because the passage does not state that assault is a lesser form of lethal force, only that an assault can use lethal force, or alternatively, lethal force can be utilized to counter a dangerous assault. Choice *C* is incorrect because the passage is informative and does not have a set agenda. Finally, Choice *D* is incorrect because although the author uses an example in order to explain assault, it is not indicated that this is the author's personal account.

36. C: If the man being attacked in an alley by another man with a knife used self-defense by lethal force, it would not be considered illegal. The presence of a deadly weapon indicates mal-intent and because the individual is isolated in an alley, lethal force in self-defense may be the only way to preserve his life. Choices *A* and *B* can be ruled out because in these situations, no one is in danger of immediate death or bodily harm by someone else. Choice *D* is an assault and does exhibit intent to harm, but this situation isn't severe enough to merit lethal force; there is no intent to kill.

37. B: As discussed in the second passage, there are several forms of assault, like assault with a deadly weapon, verbal assault, or threatening posture or language. Choice *A* is incorrect because the author does mention what the charges are on assaults; therefore, we cannot assume that they are more or less than unnecessary use of force charges. Choice *C* is incorrect because anyone is capable of assault; the author does not state that one group of people cannot commit assault. Choice *D* is incorrect because assault is never justified. Self-defense resulting in lethal force can be justified.

38. D: The use of lethal force is not evaluated on the intent of the user, but rather on the severity of the primary attack that warranted self-defense. This statement most undermines the last part of the passage because it directly contradicts how the law evaluates the use of lethal force. Choices *A* and *B* are stated in the paragraph, so they do not undermine the explanation from the author. Choice *C* does not necessarily undermine the passage, but it does not support the passage either. It is more of an opinion that does not offer strength or weakness to the explanation.

39. C: An assault with deadly intent can lead to an individual using lethal force to preserve their well-being. Choice *C* is correct because it clearly establishes what both assault and lethal force are and gives the specific way in which the two concepts meet. Choice *A* is incorrect because lethal force doesn't necessarily result in assault. This is also why Choice *B* is incorrect. Not all assaults would necessarily be life-threatening to the point where lethal force is needed for self-defense. Choice *D* is compelling but ultimately too vague; the statement touches on aspects of the two ideas but fails to present the concrete way in which the two are connected to each other.

40. A: Both passages open by defining a legal concept and then continue to describe situations in order to further explain the concept. Choice *D* is incorrect because while the passages utilize examples to help explain the concepts discussed, the author doesn't indicate that they are specific court cases. It's also clear that the passages don't open with examples, but instead, they begin by defining the terms addressed in each passage. This eliminates Choice *B*, and ultimately reveals Choice *A* to be the correct answer. Choice *A* accurately outlines the way both passages are structured. Because the passages follow a nearly identical structure, the Choice *C* can easily be ruled out.

41. C: *Extraneous* most nearly means *superfluous*, or *trivial*. Choice *A*, *indispensable*, is incorrect because it means the opposite of *extraneous*. Choice *B*, *bewildering*, means *confusing* and is not relevant to the context of the sentence. Finally, Choice *D* is wrong because although the prefix of the word is the same, *ex-*, the word *exuberant* means *elated* or *enthusiastic*, and is irrelevant to the context of the sentence.

42. A: The author's purpose is to bring to light an alternative view on human perception by examining the role of technology in human understanding. This is a challenging question because the author's purpose is somewhat open-ended. The author concludes by stating that the questions regarding human perception and observation can be approached from many angles. Thus, the author does not seem to be attempting to prove one thing or another. Choice *B* is clearly wrong because we cannot know for certain whether the electron experiment is the latest discovery in astroparticle physics because no date is given. Choice *C* is a broad generalization that does not reflect accurately on the writer's views. While the author does appear to reflect on opposing views of human understanding (Choice *D*), the best answer is Choice *A*.

43. C: It presents a problem, explains the details of that problem, and then ends with more inquiry. The beginning of this paragraph literally "presents a conundrum," explains the problem of partial understanding, and then ends with more questions, or inquiry. There is no solution offered in this paragraph, making Choices *A and B* incorrect. Choice *D* is incorrect because the paragraph does not begin with a definition.

44. D: Looking back in the text, the author describes that classical philosophy holds that understanding can be reached by careful observation. This will not work if they are overly invested or biased in their pursuit. Choices *A*, *B*, and *C* are in no way related and are completely unnecessary. A specific theory is not necessary to understanding, according to classical philosophy mentioned by the author.

45. B: The electrons passed through both holes and then onto the plate. Choices *A* and *C* are wrong because such movement is not mentioned at all in the text. In the passage the author says that electrons that were physically observed appeared to pass through one hole or another. Remember, the electrons that were observed doing this were described as acting like particles. Therefore, Choice *D* is wrong. Recall that the plate actually recorded electrons passing through both holes simultaneously and hitting the plate. This behavior, the electron activity that wasn't seen by humans, was characteristic of waves. Thus, Choice *B* is the right answer.

46. C: The author uses "gravity" to demonstrate an example of natural phenomena humans discovered and understand without the use of tools or machines. Choice *A* mirrors the language in the beginning of the paragraph but is incorrect in its intent. Choice *B* is incorrect; the paragraph mentions nothing of "not knowing the true nature of gravity." Choice *D* is incorrect as well. There is no mention of an "alternative solution" to new technology in this paragraph.

Math

Numbers and Operations

Properties of Operations with Real Numbers, Including Rational and Irrational Numbers

The mathematical number system is made up of two general types of numbers: real and complex. *Real numbers* are those that are used in normal settings, while *complex numbers* are those composed of both a real number and an imaginary one. Imaginary numbers are the result of taking the square root of -1, and $\sqrt{-1} = i$.

The real number system is often explained using a Venn diagram similar to the one below. After a number has been labeled as a real number, further classification occurs when considering the other groups in this diagram. If a number is a never-ending, non-repeating decimal, it falls in the irrational category. Otherwise, it is rational. More information on these types of numbers is provided in the previous section. Furthermore, if a number does not have a fractional part, it is classified as an integer, such as -2, 75, or zero. Whole numbers are an even smaller group that only includes positive integers and zero. The last group of natural numbers is made up of only positive integers, such as 2, 56, or 12.

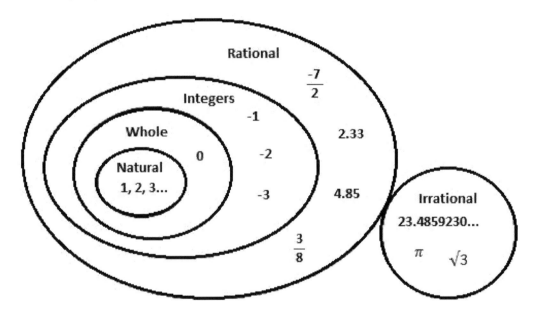

Real numbers can be compared and ordered using the number line. If a number falls to the left on the real number line, it is less than a number on the right. For example, $-2 < 5$ because -2 falls to the left of zero, and 5 falls to the right. Numbers to the left of zero are negative while those to the right are positive.

Complex numbers are made up of the sum of a real number and an imaginary number. Some examples of complex numbers include $6 + 2i$, $5 - 7i$, and $-3 + 12i$. Adding and subtracting complex numbers is similar to collecting like terms. The real numbers are added together, and the imaginary numbers are added together. For example, if the problem asks to simplify the expression $6 + 2i - 3 + 7i$, the 6 and (-3) are combined to make 3, and the $2i$ and $7i$ combine to make $9i$. Multiplying and dividing complex numbers is similar to working with exponents. One rule to remember when multiplying is that $i \times i =$

−1. For example, if a problem asks to simplify the expression $4i(3 + 7i)$, the $4i$ should be distributed throughout the 3 and the $7i$. This leaves the final expression $12i − 28$. The 28 is negative because $i \times i$ results in a negative number. The last type of operation to consider with complex numbers is the conjugate. The *conjugate* of a complex number is a technique used to change the complex number into a real number. For example, the conjugate of $4 − 3i$ is $4 + 3i$. Multiplying $(4 − 3i)(4 + 3i)$ results in $16 + 12i − 12i + 9$, which has a final answer of $16 + 9 = 25$.

The order of operations—PEMDAS—simplifies longer expressions with real or imaginary numbers. Each operation is listed in the order of how they should be completed in a problem containing more than one operation. Parenthesis can also mean grouping symbols, such as brackets and absolute value. Then, exponents are calculated. Multiplication and division should be completed from left to right, and addition and subtraction should be completed from left to right. The following shows step-by-step how an expression is simplified using the order of operations:

$$25 \div (8 − 3)^2 − 1$$

$$25 \div (5)^2 − 1$$

$$25 \div 25 − 1$$

$$1 − 1$$

$$0$$

Simplification of another type of expression occurs when radicals are involved. As explained previously, root is another word for radical. For example, the following expression is a radical that can be simplified: $\sqrt{24x^2}$. First, the number must be factored out to the highest perfect square. Any perfect square can be taken out of a radical. Twenty-four can be factored into 4 and 6, and 4 can be taken out of the radical. $\sqrt{4} = 2$ can be taken out, and 6 stays underneath. If $x > 0$, x can be taken out of the radical because it is a perfect square. The simplified radical is $2x\sqrt{6}$. An approximation can be found using a calculator.

There are also properties of numbers that are true for certain operations. The *commutative* property allows the order of the terms in an expression to change while keeping the same final answer. Both addition and multiplication can be completed in any order and still obtain the same result. However, order does matter in subtraction and division. The *associative* property allows any terms to be "associated" by parenthesis and retain the same final answer. For example, $(4 + 3) + 5 = 4 + (3 + 5)$. Both addition and multiplication are associative; however, subtraction and division do not hold this property. The *distributive* property states that $a(b + c) = ab + ac$. It is a property that involves both addition and multiplication, and the a is distributed onto each term inside the parentheses.

Integers can be factored into prime numbers. To *factor* is to express as a product. For example, $6 = 3 \times 2$, and $6 = 6 \times 1$. Both are factorizations, but the expression involving the factors of 3 and 2 is known as a *prime factorization* because it is factored into a product of two *prime numbers*—integers which do not have any factors other than themselves and 1. A *composite number* is a positive integer that can be divided into at least one other integer other than itself and 1, such as 6. Integers that have a factor of 2 are even, and if they are not divisible by 2, they are odd. Finally, a *multiple* of a number is the product of that number and a counting number—also known as a *natural number*. For example, some multiples of 4 are 4, 8, 12, 16, etc.

Properties of Rational and Irrational Numbers

All real numbers can be separated into two groups: rational and irrational numbers. *Rational numbers* are any numbers that can be written as a fraction, such as $\frac{1}{3}, \frac{7}{4}$, and -25. Alternatively, *irrational numbers* are those that cannot be written as a fraction, such as numbers with never-ending, non-repeating decimal values. Many irrational numbers result from taking roots, such as $\sqrt{2}$ or $\sqrt{3}$. An irrational number may be written as:

$$34.5684952\ldots$$

The ellipsis (…) represents the line of numbers after the decimal that does not repeat and is never-ending.

When rational and irrational numbers interact, there are different types of number outcomes. For example, when adding or multiplying two rational numbers, the result is a rational number. No matter what two fractions are added or multiplied together, the result can always be written as a fraction. The following expression shows two rational numbers multiplied together:

$$\frac{3}{8} \times \frac{4}{7} = \frac{12}{56}$$

The product of these two fractions is another fraction that can be simplified to $\frac{3}{14}$.

As another interaction, rational numbers added to irrational numbers will always result in irrational numbers. No part of any fraction can be added to a never-ending, non-repeating decimal to make a rational number. The same result is true when multiplying a rational and irrational number. Taking a fractional part of a never-ending, non-repeating decimal will always result in another never-ending, non-repeating decimal. An example of the product of rational and irrational numbers is shown in the following expression: $2 \times \sqrt{7}$.

The last type of interaction concerns two irrational numbers, where the sum or product may be rational or irrational depending on the numbers being used. The following expression shows a rational sum from two irrational numbers:

$$\sqrt{3} + \left(6 - \sqrt{3}\right) = 6$$

The product of two irrational numbers can be rational or irrational. A rational result can be seen in the following expression:

$$\sqrt{2} \times \sqrt{8} = \sqrt{2 \times 8} = \sqrt{16} = 4$$

An irrational result can be seen in the following:

$$\sqrt{3} \times \sqrt{2} = \sqrt{6}$$

Rewriting Expressions Involving Radicals and Rational Exponents Using the Properties of Exponents

Exponents are used in mathematics to express a number or variable multiplied by itself a certain number of times. For example, x^3 means x is multiplied by itself three times. In this expression, x is called the base, and 3 is the *exponent*. Exponents can be used in more complex problems when they contain fractions and negative numbers.

Fractional exponents can be explained by looking first at the inverse of exponents, which are *roots*. Given the expression x^2, the square root can be taken, $\sqrt{x^2}$, cancelling out the 2 and leaving x by itself, if x is positive. Cancellation occurs because $\sqrt{x}$ can be written with exponents, instead of roots, as $x^{\frac{1}{2}}$. The numerator of 1 is the exponent, and the denominator of 2 is called the root (which is why it's referred to as *square root*). Taking the square root of x^2 is the same as raising it to the $\frac{1}{2}$ power. Written out in mathematical form, it takes the following progression:

$$\sqrt{x^2} = (x^2)^{\frac{1}{2}} = x$$

From properties of exponents, $2 \times \frac{1}{2} = 1$ is the actual exponent of x. Another example can be seen with $x^{\frac{4}{7}}$. The variable x, raised to four-sevenths, is equal to the seventh root of x to the fourth power: $\sqrt[7]{x^4}$. In general,

$$x^{\frac{1}{n}} = \sqrt[n]{x}$$

and

$$x^{\frac{m}{n}} = \sqrt[n]{x^m}$$

Negative exponents also involve fractions. Whereas y^3 can also be rewritten as $\frac{y^3}{1}$, y^{-3} can be rewritten as $\frac{1}{y^3}$. A negative exponent means the exponential expression must be moved to the opposite spot in a fraction to make the exponent positive. If the negative appears in the numerator, it moves to the denominator. If the negative appears in the denominator, it is moved to the numerator. In general, $a^{-n} = \frac{1}{a^n}$, and a^{-n} and a^n are reciprocals.

Take, for example, the following expression:

$$\frac{a^{-4}b^2}{c^{-5}}$$

Since a is raised to the negative fourth power, it can be moved to the denominator. Since c is raised to the negative fifth power, it can be moved to the numerator. The b variable is raised to the positive second power, so it does not move.

The simplified expression is as follows:

$$\frac{b^2c^5}{a^4}$$

In mathematical expressions containing exponents and other operations, the order of operations must be followed. *PEMDAS* states that exponents are calculated after any parenthesis and grouping symbols, but before any multiplication, division, addition, and subtraction.

Scientific Notation

Scientific Notation is used to represent numbers that are either very small or very large. For example, the distance to the sun is approximately 150,000,000,000 meters. Instead of writing this number with so many zeros, it can be written in scientific notation as 1.5×10^{11} meters. The same is true for very small numbers, but the exponent becomes negative. If the mass of a human cell is 0.000000000001 kilograms, that measurement can be easily represented by 1.0×10^{-12} kilograms. In both situations, scientific notation makes the measurement easier to read and understand. Each number is translated to an expression with one digit in the tens place times an expression corresponding to the zeros.

When two measurements are given and both involve scientific notation, it is important to know how these interact with each other:

- In addition and subtraction, the exponent on the ten must be the same before any operations are performed on the numbers. For example, $(1.3 \times 10^4) + (3.0 \times 10^3)$ cannot be added until one of the exponents on the ten is changed. The 3.0×10^3 can be changed to 0.3×10^4, then the 1.3 and 0.3 can be added. The answer comes out to be 1.6×10^4.

- For multiplication, the first numbers can be multiplied and then the exponents on the tens can be added. Once an answer is formed, it may have to be converted into scientific notation again depending on the change that occurred.

- The following is an example of multiplication with scientific notation:

$$(4.5 \times 10^3) \times (3.0 \times 10^{-5}) = 13.5 \times 10^{-2}$$

- Since this answer is not in scientific notation, the decimal is moved over to the left one unit, and 1 is added to the ten's exponent. This results in the final answer: 1.35×10^{-1}.

- For division, the first numbers are divided, and the exponents on the tens are subtracted. Again, the answer may need to be converted into scientific notation form, depending on the type of changes that occurred during the problem.

- *Order of magnitude* relates to scientific notation and is the total count of powers of 10 in a number. For example, there are 6 orders of magnitude in 1,000,000. If a number is raised by an order of magnitude, it is multiplied times 10. Order of magnitude can be helpful in estimating results using very large or small numbers. An answer should make sense in terms of its order of magnitude.

- For example, if area is calculated using two dimensions with 6 orders of magnitude, because area involves multiplication, the answer should have around 12 orders of magnitude. Also, answers can be estimated by rounding to the largest place value in each number. For example, 5,493,302×2,523,100 can be estimated by 5×3 = 15 with 6 orders of magnitude.

Reasoning Quantitatively and Using Units to Solve Problems

Dimensional analysis is the process of converting between different units using equivalent measurement statements. For example, running a 5K is the same as running approximately 3.1 miles. This conversion can be found by knowing that 1 kilometer is equal to approximately 0.62 miles.

The following calculation shows how to convert kilometers into miles. The original units need to be opposite one another in each of the two fractions: one in the original amount and one in the denominator of the conversion factor. This specific example consists of 5 km being multiplied times the conversion factor .62 mi/km. By design, quantities in kilometers are opposite one another and therefore cancel, leaving 3.11 miles as the converted result.

$$5km \times \left(\frac{0.62 miles}{1km}\right) = 3.11 \; miles$$

Units are also important throughout formulas in calculating quantities such as volume and area. To find the volume of a pyramid, the following formula is used: $V = \frac{1}{3}Bh$. B is the area of the base, and h is the height. In the example shown below, two of the same type of dimension are composed of two different units. All dimensions must be converted to the same units before plugging values into the formula for volume.

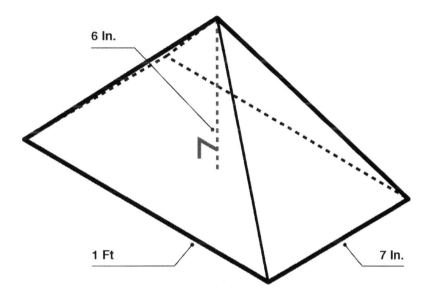

In this case, all lengths will be converted to inches. To find the area of the base, it's necessary to convert 1 ft. to 12 inches. Then, the area of the base can be calculated as $B = 12 \; in \times 7 \; in = 84 \; in^2$. B can then be substituted into the volume formula as follows: $V = \frac{1}{3}(84in^2)(6in) = 168 \; in^3$.

Formulas are a common situation in which units need to be interpreted and used. However, graphs can also carry meaning through units. The following graph is an example. It represents a graph of the position of an object over time. The m axis represents the number of meters the object is from the starting point at time s, in seconds. Interpreting this graph, the origin shows that at time zero seconds, the object is zero meters away from the starting point. As the time increases to one second, the position increases to five meters away. This trend continues until 6 seconds, where the object is 30 meters away from the starting position. After this point in time—since the graph remains horizontal from 6 to 10 seconds—the object must have stopped moving.

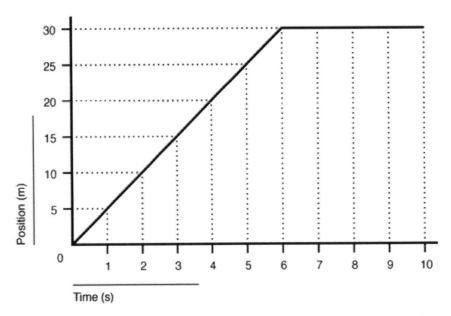

In each of the previous problem examples, the units were important to the answer. When solving problems with units, it's important to consider the reasonableness of the answer. If conversions are used, it's helpful to have an estimated value to compare the final answer to. This way, if the final answer is too distant from the estimate, it will be obvious that a mistake was made.

Choosing a Level of Accuracy Appropriate to Limitations on Measurement

Precision and accuracy are used to describe groups of measurements. *Precision* describes a group of measures that are very close together, regardless of whether the measures are close to the true value. *Accuracy* describes how close the measures are to the true value. The following graphic illustrates the different combinations that may occur with different groups of measures:

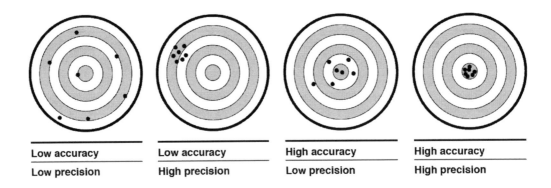

Since accuracy refers to the closeness of a value to the true measurement, the level of accuracy depends on the object measured and the instrument used to measure it. This will vary depending on the situation. If measuring the mass of a set of dictionaries, kilograms may be used as the units. In this case, it is not vitally important to have a high level of accuracy. If the measurement is a few grams away from the true value, the discrepancy might not make a big difference in the problem.

In a different situation, the level of accuracy may be more significant. Pharmacists need to be sure they are very accurate in their measurements of medicines that they give to patients. In this case, the level of accuracy is vitally important and not something to be estimated. In the dictionary situation, the measurements were given as whole numbers in kilograms. In the pharmacist's situation, the measurements for medicine must be taken to the milligram and sometimes further, depending on the type of medicine.

When considering the accuracy of measurements, the error in each measurement can be shown as absolute and relative. *Absolute error* tells the actual difference between the measured value and the true value. The *relative error* tells how large the error is in relation to the true value. There may be two problems where the absolute error of the measurements is 10 grams. For one problem, this may mean the relative error is very small because the measured value is 14,990 grams, and the true value is 15,000 grams. Ten grams in relation to the true value of 15,000 is small: 0.06%. For the other problem, the measured value is 290 grams, and the true value is 300 grams. In this case, the 10-gram absolute error means a high relative error because the true value is smaller. The relative error is 10/300 = 0.03, or 3%.

Solving Multistep Real-World and Mathematical Problems Involving Rational Numbers in Any Form

*Ratio*s are used to show the relationship between two quantities. The ratio of oranges to apples in the grocery store may be 3 to 2. That means that for every 3 oranges, there are 2 apples. This comparison can be expanded to represent the actual number of oranges and apples. Another example may be the number of boys to girls in a math class. If the ration of boys to girls is given as 2 to 5, that means there are 2 boys to every 5 girls in the class. Ratios can also be compared if the units in each ratio are the same. The ratio of boys to girls in the math class can be compared to the ratio of boys to girls in a science class by stating which ratio is higher and which is lower.

Rates are used to compare two quantities with different units. *Unit rates* are the simplest form of rate. With unit rates, the denominator in the comparison of two units is one. For example, if someone can type at a rate of 1000 words in 5 minutes, then his or her unit rate for typing is $\frac{1000}{5} = 200$ words in one minute or 200 words per minute. Any rate can be converted into a unit rate by dividing to make the denominator one. 1000 words in 5 minutes has been converted into the unit rate of 200 words per minute.

Ratios and rates can be used together to convert rates into different units. For example, if someone is driving 50 kilometers per hour, that rate can be converted into miles per hour by using a ratio known as the *conversion factor*. Since the given value contains kilometers and the final answer needs to be in miles, the ratio relating miles to kilometers needs to be used. There are 0.62 miles in 1 kilometer. This, written as a ratio and in fraction form, is

$$\frac{0.62 \; miles}{1 \; km}$$

To convert 50km/hour into miles per hour, the following conversion needs to be set up:

$$\frac{50 \; km}{hour} \times \frac{0.62 \; miles}{1 \; km} = 31 \; miles \; per \; hour$$

The ratio between two similar geometric figures is called the *scale factor*. In the following example, there are two similar triangles. The scale factor from figure A to figure B is 2 because the length of the corresponding side of the larger triangle, 14, is twice the corresponding side on the smaller triangle, 7.

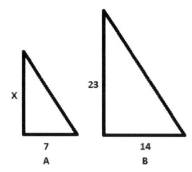

This scale factor can also be used to find the value of X. Since the scale factor from small to large is 2, the larger number, 23, can be divided by 2 to find the missing side: X=11.5. The scale factor can also be represented in the equation $2A = B$ because two times the lengths of A gives the corresponding lengths of B. This is the idea behind similar triangles.

Much like a scale factor can be written using an equation like $2A = B$, a *proportional relationship* is represented by the equation $Y = kX$. X and Y are proportional because as values in X increase, the values in Y also increase. A relationship that is inversely proportional can be represented by the equation $Y = \frac{k}{x}$, where the value of Y decreases as the value of X increases and vice versa. The following graph represents these two types of relationships between x and y. The grey line represents a proportional relationship because the y-values increase as the x-values increase. The black line represents an inversely-proportional relationship because the y-values decrease as the x-values increase.

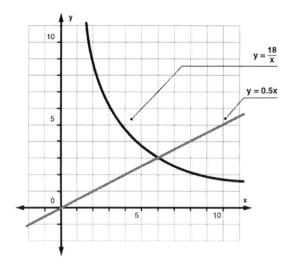

Proportional reasoning can be used to solve problems involving ratios, percentages, and averages. Ratios can be used in setting up proportions and solving them to find unknowns. For example, if someone averages 10 pages of math homework completed in 3 nights, how long would it take him or

80

her to complete 22 pages? Both ratios can be written as fractions. The second ratio would contain the unknown. The following proportion represents this problem where x is the unknown number of nights:

$$\frac{10 \; pages}{3 \; nights} = \frac{22 \; pages}{x \; nights}$$

Solving this proportion entails cross-multiplying and results in the following equation: $10x = 22 \times 3$. Simplifying and solving for x results in the exact solution: $x = 6.6 \; nights$. The result would be rounded up to 7 because the homework would be actually be completed on the 7th night.

The following problem uses ratios involving percentages:

If 20% of the class is girls and 30 students are in the class, how many girls are in the class?

To set up this problem, it is helpful to use the common proportion: $\frac{\%}{100} = \frac{is}{of}$. Within the proportion, % is the percentage of girls, 100 is the total percentage of the class, *is* is the number of girls, and *of* is the total number of students in the class. Most percentage problems can be written using this language. To solve this problem, the proportion should be set up as $\frac{20}{100} = \frac{x}{30}$, then solved for x. Cross-multiplying results in the equation $20 \times 30 = 100x$, which results in the solution $x = 6$. There are 6 girls in the class.

Problems involving volume, length, and other units can also be solved using ratios. If the following graphic of a cone is given, the problem may ask for the volume to be found.

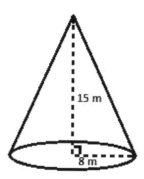

15 m

8 m

Referring to the formulas provided on the test, the volume of a cone is given as: $V = \pi r^2 \frac{h}{3}$, where r is the radius, and h is the height. Plugging $r = 8$ and $h = 15$ from the graphic into the formula, the following is obtained: $V = \pi(8^2)\frac{15}{3}$. Therefore, volume of the cone is found to be 1005.3m³. Sometimes, answers in different units are sought. If this problem wanted the answer in liters, 1005.3m³ would need to be converted. Using the equivalence statement 1m³ = 1000L, the following ratio would be used to solve for liters: $1005.3m^3 \times \frac{1000L}{1m^3}$. Cubic meters in the numerator and denominator cancel each other out, and the answer is converted to 1,005,300 liters, or 1.0053×10^6 L.

Other conversions can also be made between different given and final units. If the temperature in a pool is 30°C, what is the temperature of the pool in degrees Fahrenheit? To convert these units, an equation is used relating Celsius to Fahrenheit. The following equation is used: $T_{°F} = 1.8T_{°C} + 32$. Plugging in the given temperature and solving the equation for T yields the result: $T_{°F} = 1.8(30) + 32 = 86°F$. Both units in the metric system and U.S. customary system are widely used.

Algebra

Interpreting Parts of an Expression, Such as Quadratic, Factors, and Coefficients in Terms of its Context

Algebraic expressions are built out of monomials. A *monomial* is a variable raised to some power multiplied by a constant: ax^n, where a is any constant and n is a whole number. A constant is also a monomial.

A *polynomial* is a sum of monomials. Examples of polynomials include $3x^4 + 2x^2 - x - 3$ and $\frac{4}{5}x^3$. The latter is also a monomial. If the highest power of x is 1, the polynomial is called *linear*. If the highest power of x is 2, it is called *quadratic*.

Algebraic Functions

A function is called *algebraic* if it is built up from polynomials by adding, subtracting, multiplying, dividing, and taking radicals. This means that, for example, the variable can never appear in an exponent. Thus, polynomials and rational functions are algebraic, but exponential functions are not algebraic. It turns out that logarithms and trigonometric functions are not algebraic either.

A function of the form $f(x) = a_n x^n + a_{n-1} x^{n-1} + a_{n-2} x^{n-2} + \cdots + a_1 x + a_0$ is called a *polynomial function*. The value of n is called the *degree* of the polynomial. In the case where $n = 1$, it is called a *linear function*. In the case where $n = 2$, it is called a *quadratic function*. In the case where $n = 3$, it is called a *cubic function*.

When n is even, the polynomial is called *even*, and not all real numbers will be in its range. When n is odd, the polynomial is called *odd*, and the range includes all real numbers.

The graph of a quadratic function $f(x) = ax^2 + bx + c$ will be a parabola. To see whether or not the parabola opens up or down, it's necessary to check the coefficient of x^2, which is the value a.

If the coefficient is positive, then the parabola opens upward. If the coefficient is negative, then the parabola opens downward.

The quantity $D = b^2 - 4ac$ is called the *discriminant* of the parabola. If the discriminant is positive, then the parabola has two real zeros. If the discriminant is negative, then it has no real zeros.

If the discriminant is zero, then the parabola's highest or lowest point is on the x-axis, and it has a single real zero.

The highest or lowest point of the parabola is called the *vertex*. The coordinates of the vertex are given by the point $(-\frac{b}{2a}, -\frac{D}{4a})$. The roots of a quadratic function can be found with the quadratic formula, which is $x = \frac{-b \pm \sqrt{b^2 - 4ac}}{2a}$.

A *rational function* is a function $f(x) = \frac{p(x)}{q(x)}$, where p and q are both polynomials. The domain of f will be all real numbers except the (real) roots of q.

At these roots, the graph of f will have a *vertical asymptote*, unless they are also roots of p. Here is an example to consider:

$$p(x) = p_n x^n + p_{n-1} x^{n-1} + p_{n-2} x^{n-2} + \cdots + p_1 x + p_0$$

$$q(x) = q_m x^m + q_{m-1} x^{m-1} + q_{m-2} x^{m-2} + \cdots + q_1 x + q_0$$

When the degree of p is less than the degree of q, there will be a horizontal asymptote of $y = 0$. If p and q have the same degree, there will be a horizontal asymptote of $y = \frac{p_n}{q_n}$. If the degree of p is exactly one greater than the degree of q, then f will have an oblique asymptote along the line $y = \frac{p_n}{q_{n-1}} x + \frac{p_{n-1}}{q_{n-1}}$.

Exponential Functions

An *exponential function* is a function of the form $f(x) = b^x$, where b is a positive real number other than 1. In such a function, b is called the *base*.

The *domain* of an exponential function is all real numbers, and the *range* is all positive real numbers. There will always be a horizontal asymptote of $y = 0$ on one side. If b is greater than 1, then the graph will be increasing moving to the right. If b is less than 1, then the graph will be decreasing moving to the right. Exponential functions are one-to-one. The basic exponential function graph will go through the point (0,1).

Example
Solve $5^{x+1} = 25$.

Get the x out of the exponent by rewriting the equation $5^{x+1} = 5^2$ so that both sides have a base of 5.

Since the bases are the same, the exponents must be equal to each other.

This leaves $x + 1 = 2$ or $x = 1$.

To check the answer, the x-value of 1 can be substituted back into the original equation.

Performing Arithmetic Operations on Polynomials and Rational Expressions

Addition and subtraction operations can be performed on polynomials with like terms. *Like terms* refers to terms that have the same variable and exponent. The two following polynomials can be added together by collecting like terms:

$$(x^2 + 3x - 4) + (4x^2 - 7x + 8)$$

The x^2 terms can be added as $x^2 + 4x^2 = 5x^2$. The x terms can be added as $3x + -7x = -4x$, and the constants can be added as $-4 + 8 = 4$. The following expression is the result of the addition:

$$5x^2 - 4x + 4$$

When subtracting polynomials, the same steps are followed, only subtracting like terms together.

Multiplication of polynomials can also be performed. Given the two polynomials, $(y^3 - 4)$ and $(x^2 + 8x - 7)$, each term in the first polynomial must be multiplied by each term in the second polynomial. The steps to multiply each term in the given example are as follows:

$$(y^3 \times x^2) + (y^3 \times 8x) + (y^3 \times -7) + (-4 \times x^2) + (-4 \times 8x) + (-4 \times -7)$$

Simplifying each multiplied part, yields:

$$x^2 y^3 + 8xy^3 - 7y^3 - 4x^2 - 32x + 28$$

None of the terms can be combined because there are no like terms in the final expression. Any polynomials can be multiplied by each other by following the same set of steps, then collecting like terms at the end.

Polynomial Identities

Difference of squares refers to a binomial composed of the difference of two squares. For example, $a^2 - b^2$ is a difference of squares. It can be written $(a)^2 - (b)^2$, and it can be factored into $(a - b)(a + b)$. Recognizing the difference of squares allows the expression to be rewritten easily because of the form it takes. For some expressions, factoring consists of more than one step. When factoring, it's important to always check to make sure that the result cannot be factored further. If it can, then the expression should be split further. If it cannot be, the factoring step is complete, and the expression is completely factored.

A sum and difference of cubes is another way to factor a polynomial expression. When the polynomial takes the form of addition or subtraction of two terms that can be written as a cube, a formula is given. The following graphic shows the factorization of a difference of cubes:

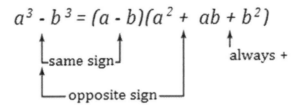

This form of factoring can be useful in finding the zeros of a function of degree 3. For example, when solving $x^3 - 27 = 0$, this rule needs to be used. $x^3 - 27$ is first written as the difference two cubes, $(x)^3 - (3)^3$ and then factored into $(x - 3)(x^2 + 3x + 9)$. This expression may not be factored any further. Each factor is then set equal to zero. Therefore, one solution is found to be $x = 3$, and the other two solutions must be found using the quadratic formula. A sum of squares would have a similar process. The formula for factoring a sum of squares is:

$$a^3 + b^3 = (a + b)(a^2 - ab + b^2)$$

The opposite of factoring is multiplying. Multiplying a square of a binomial involves the following rules:

$$(a + b)^2 = a^2 + 2ab + b^2$$

$$(a - b)^2 = a^2 - 2ab + b^2$$

The binomial theorem for expansion can be used when the exponent on a binomial is larger than 2, and the multiplication would take a long time. The binomial theorem is given as:

$$(a + b)^n = \sum_{k=0}^{n} \binom{n}{k} a^{n-k} b^k$$

$$\text{where} \quad \binom{n}{k} = \frac{n!}{k!(n-k)!}$$

The *Remainder Theorem* can be helpful when evaluating polynomial functions $P(x)$ for a given value of x. A polynomial can be divided by $(x - a)$, if there is a remainder of 0. This also means that $P(a) = 0$ and $(x - a)$ is a factor of $P(x)$. In a similar sense, if P is evaluated at any other number b, $P(b)$ is equal to the remainder of dividing $P(x)$ by $(x - b)$. For example, consider $P(x) = x^3 - 7x - 6$.

$$P(4) = 30 \text{ because}$$

$$
\require{enclose}
\begin{array}{r}
x^2 + 4x + 9 \\
x - 4 \enclose{longdiv}{x^3 + 0x^2 - 7x - 6} \\
\underline{x^3 + 4x^2} \\
4x^2 - 7x - 6 \\
\underline{4x^2 + 16x} \\
9x - 6 \\
\underline{9x + 36} \\
30
\end{array}
$$

Rational Expressions

A fraction, or ratio, wherein each part is a polynomial, defines *rational expressions*. Some examples include $\frac{2x+6}{x}$, $\frac{1}{x^2-4x+8}$, and $\frac{z^2}{x+5}$. Exponents on the variables are restricted to whole numbers, which means roots and negative exponents are not included in rational expressions.

Rational expressions can be transformed by factoring. For example, the expression $\frac{x^2-5x+6}{(x-3)}$ can be rewritten by factoring the numerator to obtain $\frac{(x-3)(x-2)}{(x-3)}$. Therefore, the common binomial $(x - 3)$ can cancel so that the simplified expression is $\frac{(x-2)}{1} = (x - 2)$.

Additionally, other rational expressions can be rewritten to take on different forms. Some may be factorable in themselves, while others can be transformed through arithmetic operations. Rational expressions are closed under addition, subtraction, multiplication, and division by a nonzero expression. *Closed* means that if any one of these operations is performed on a rational expression, the result will still be a rational expression. The set of all real numbers is another example of a set closed under all four operations.

Adding and subtracting rational expressions is based on the same concepts as adding and subtracting simple fractions. For both concepts, the denominators must be the same for the operation to take place. For example, here are two rational expressions:

$$\frac{x^3 - 4}{(x - 3)} + \frac{x + 8}{(x - 3)}$$

Since the denominators are both $(x - 3)$, the numerators can be combined by collecting like terms to form:

$$\frac{x^3 + x + 4}{(x - 3)}$$

If the denominators are different, they need to be made common (the same) by using the Least Common Denominator (LCD). Each denominator needs to be factored, and the LCD contains each factor that appears in any one denominator the greatest number of times it appears in any denominator. The original expressions need to be multiplied times a form of 1, which will turn each denominator into the LCD. This process is like adding fractions with unlike denominators. It is also important when working with rational expressions to define what value of the variable makes the denominator zero. For this particular value, the expression is undefined.

Multiplication of rational expressions is performed like multiplication of fractions. The numerators are multiplied; then, the denominators are multiplied. The final fraction is then simplified. The expressions are simplified by factoring and cancelling out common terms. In the following example, the numerator of the second expression can be factored first to simplify the expression before multiplying:

$$\frac{x^2}{(x - 4)} \times \frac{x^2 - x - 12}{2}$$

$$\frac{x^2}{(x - 4)} \times \frac{(x - 4)(x + 3)}{2}$$

The $(x - 4)$ on the top and bottom cancel out:

$$\frac{x^2}{1} \times \frac{(x + 3)}{2}$$

Then multiplication is performed, resulting in:

$$\frac{x^3 + 3x^2}{2}$$

Dividing rational expressions is similar to the division of fractions, where division turns into multiplying by a reciprocal. The following expression can be rewritten as a multiplication problem:

$$\frac{x^2 - 3x + 7}{x - 4} \div \frac{x^2 - 5x + 3}{x - 4}$$

$$\frac{x^2 - 3x + 7}{x - 4} \times \frac{x - 4}{x^2 - 5x + 3}$$

The $x - 4$ cancels out, leaving:

$$\frac{x^2 - 3x + 7}{x^2 - 5x + 3}$$

The final answers should always be completely simplified. If a function is composed of a rational expression, the zeros of the graph can be found from setting the polynomial in the numerator as equal to zero and solving. The values that make the denominator equal to zero will either exist on the graph as a hole or a vertical asymptote.

Writing Expressions in Equivalent Forms to Solve Problems and Factoring a Quadratic Expression to Reveal the Zeros of the Function it Defines

Algebraic expressions are made up of numbers, variables, and combinations of the two, using mathematical operations. Expressions can be rewritten based on their factors. For example, the expression $6x + 4$ can be rewritten as $2(3x + 2)$ because 2 is a factor of both $6x$ and 4. More complex expressions can also be rewritten based on their factors. The expression $x^4 - 16$ can be rewritten as $(x^2 - 4)(x^2 + 4)$. This is a different type of factoring, where a difference of squares is factored into a sum and difference of the same two terms. With some expressions, the factoring process is simple and only leads to a different way to represent the expression. With others, factoring and rewriting the expression leads to more information about the given problem.

In the following quadratic equation, factoring the binomial leads to finding the zeros of the function:

$$x^2 - 5x + 6 = y$$

This equations factors into $(x - 3)(x - 2) = y$, where 2 and 3 are found to be the zeros of the function when y is set equal to zero. The zeros of any function are the x-values where the graph of the function on the coordinate plane crosses the x-axis.

Factoring an equation is a simple way to rewrite the equation and find the zeros, but factoring is not possible for every quadratic. Completing the square is one way to find zeros when factoring is not an option. The following equation cannot be factored: $x^2 + 10x - 9 = 0$. The first step in this method is to move the constant to the right side of the equation, making it $x^2 + 10x = 9$. Then, the coefficient of x is divided by 2 and squared. This number is then added to both sides of the equation, to make the equation still true. For this example, $\left(\frac{10}{2}\right)^2 = 25$ is added to both sides of the equation to obtain:

$$x^2 + 10x + 25 = 9 + 25$$

This expression simplifies to $x^2 + 10x + 25 = 34$, which can then be factored into $(x + 5)^2 = 34$. Solving for x then involves taking the square root of both sides and subtracting 5. This leads to two zeros of the function:

$$x = \pm\sqrt{34} - 5$$

Depending on the type of answer the question seeks, a calculator may be used to find exact numbers.

Given a quadratic equation in standard form— $ax^2 + bx + c = 0$—the sign of a tells whether the function has a minimum value or a maximum value. If $a > 0$, the graph opens up and has a minimum value. If $a < 0$, the graph opens down and has a maximum value. Depending on the way the quadratic equation is written, multiplication may need to occur before a max/min value is determined.

Exponential expressions can also be rewritten, just as quadratic equations. Properties of exponents must be understood. Multiplying two exponential expressions with the same base involves adding the exponents:

$$a^m a^n = a^{m+n}$$

Dividing two exponential expressions with the same base involves subtracting the exponents:

$$\frac{a^m}{a^n} = a^{m-n}$$

Raising an exponential expression to another exponent includes multiplying the exponents:

$$(a^m)^n = a^{mn}$$

The zero power always gives a value of 1: $a^0 = 1$. Raising either a product or a fraction to a power involves distributing that power:

$$(ab)^m = a^m b^m \text{ and } \left(\frac{a}{b}\right)^m = \frac{a^m}{b^m}$$

Finally, raising a number to a negative exponent is equivalent to the reciprocal including the positive exponent:

$$a^{-m} = \frac{1}{a^m}$$

Finding the Zeros of a Function

The zeros of a function are the points where its graph crosses the x-axis. At these points, $y = 0$. One way to find the zeros is to analyze the graph. If given the graph, the x-coordinates can be found where the line crosses the x-axis. Another way to find the zeros is to set $y = 0$ in the equation and solve for x. Depending on the type of equation, this could be done by using opposite operations, by factoring the equation, by completing the square, or by using the quadratic formula. If a graph does not cross the x-axis, then the function may have complex roots.

Solving Linear Equations and Inequalities in One Variable, Including Equations with Coefficients Represented by Letters

The sum of a number and 5 is equal to 10 times the number. To find this unknown number, a simple equation can be written to represent the problem. Key words such as *sum*, *equal*, and *times* are used to form the following equation with one variable: $n + 5 = 10n$. When solving for n, opposite operations are used. First, n is subtracted from $10n$ across the equals sign, resulting in $5 = 9n$. Then, 9 is divided on both sides, leaving $n = \frac{5}{9}$. This solution can be graphed on the number line with a dot as shown below:

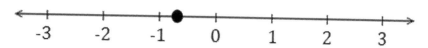

If the problem were changed to say, "The sum of a number and 5 is greater than 10 times the number," then an inequality would be used instead of an equation. Using key words again, *greater than* is represented by the symbol >. The inequality $n + 5 > 10n$ can be solved using the same techniques, resulting in $n < \frac{5}{9}$. The only time solving an inequality differs from solving an equation is when a negative number is either multiplied times or divided by each side of the inequality. The sign must be switched in this case. For this example, the graph of the solution changes to the following graph because the solution represents all real numbers less than $\frac{5}{9}$. Not included in this solution is $\frac{5}{9}$ because it is a *less than* symbol, not *equal to*.

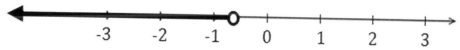

Equations and inequalities in two variables represent a relationship. Jim owns a car wash and charges $40 per car. The rent for the facility is $350 per month. An equation can be written to relate the number of cars Jim cleans to the money he makes per month. Let x represent the number of cars and y represent the profit Jim makes each month from the car wash. The equation $y = 40x - 350$ can be used to show Jim's profit or loss. Since this equation has two variables, the coordinate plane can be used to show the relationship and predict profit or loss for Jim. The following graph shows that Jim must wash at least nine cars to pay the rent, where $x = 9$. Anything nine cars and above yield a profit shown in the value on the y-axis.

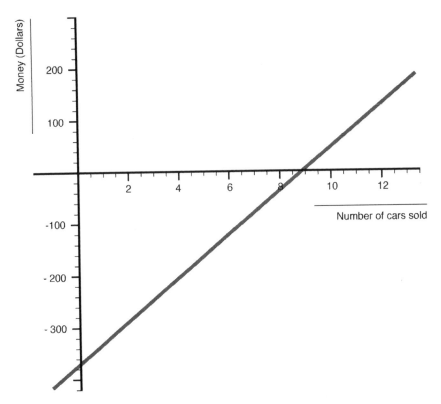

With a single equation in two variables, the solutions are limited only by the situation the equation represents. When two equations or inequalities are used, more constraints are added. For example, in a system of linear equations, there is often—although not always—only one answer. The point of intersection of two lines is the solution. For a system of inequalities, there are infinitely many answers.

The intersection of two solution sets gives the solution set of the system of inequalities. In the following graph, the darker shaded region is where two inequalities overlap. Any set of x and y found in that region satisfies both inequalities. The line with the positive slope is solid, meaning the values on that line are included in the solution.

The line with the negative slope is dotted, so the coordinates on that line are not included.

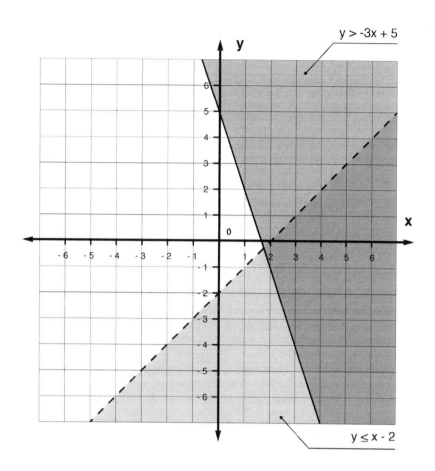

Formulas with two variables are equations used to represent a specific relationship. For example, the formula $d = rt$ represents the relationship between distance, rate, and time. If Bob travels at a rate of 35 miles per hour on his road trip from Westminster to Seneca, the formula $d = 35t$ can be used to represent his distance traveled in a specific length of time. Formulas can also be used to show different roles of the variables, transformed without any given numbers. Solving for r, the formula becomes $\frac{d}{t} = r$. The t is moved over by division so that *rate* is a function of distance and time.

Solving Equations

Solving equations in one variable is the process of The letters in an equation and any numbers attached to them are the variables, as they stand for unknown quantities that you are trying to solve for. *X* is commonly used as a variable, though any letter can be used. For example, in $3x - 7 = 20$, the variable is $3x$, and it needs to be isolated. The numbers (also called constants) are -7 and 20. That means $3x$ needs to be on one side of the equals sign (either side is fine) and all the numbers need to be on the other side of the equals sign.

To accomplish this, the equation must be manipulated by performing opposite operations of what already exists. Remember that addition and subtraction are opposites and that multiplication and division are opposites. Any action taken to one side of the equation must be taken on the other side to maintain equality.

Therefore, since the 7 is being subtracted, it can be moved to the right side of the equation by adding seven to both sides:

$$3x - 7 = 20$$

$$3x - 7 + 7 = 20 + 7$$

$$3x = 27$$

Now that the variable $3x$ is on one side and the constants (now combined into one constant) are on the other side, the 3 needs to be moved to the right side. 3 and x are being multiplied together, so 3 needs to be divided from each side.

$$\frac{3x}{3} = \frac{27}{3}$$

$$x = 9$$

Now x has been completely isolated and thus we know its value.

The solution is found to be $x = 9$. This solution can be checked for accuracy by plugging $x = 9$ in the original equation. After simplifying the equation, $20 = 20$ is found, which is a true statement:

$$3 \times 9 - 7 = 20$$

$$27 - 7 = 20$$

$$20 = 20$$

Equations that require solving for a variable (*algebraic equations*) come in many forms. Here are some more examples:

No number attached to the variable:

$$x + 8 = 20$$

$$x + 8 - 8 = 20 - 8$$

$$x = 12$$

Fraction in the variable:

$$\frac{1}{2}z + 24 = 36$$

$$\frac{1}{2}z + 24 - 24 = 36 - 24$$

$$\frac{1}{2}z = 12$$

Now we multiply the variable by its inverse:

$$\frac{2}{1} \times \frac{1}{2}z = 12 \times \frac{2}{1}$$

$$z = 24$$

Multiple examples of x:

$$14x + x - 4 = 3x + 2$$

All examples of x can be combined.

$$15x - 4 = 3x + 2$$

$$15x - 4 + 4 = 3x + 2 + 4$$

$$15x = 3x + 6$$

$$15x - 3x = 3x + 6 - 3x$$

$$12x = 6$$

$$\frac{12x}{12} = \frac{6}{12}$$

$$x = \frac{1}{2}$$

Methods for Solving Equations

Equations with one variable can be solved using the addition principle and multiplication principle. If $a = b$, then $a + c = b + c$, and $ac = bc$. Given the equation $2x - 3 = 5x + 7$, the first step is to combine the variable terms and the constant terms. Using the principles, expressions can be added and subtracted onto and off both sides of the equals sign, so the equation turns into $-10 = 3x$. Dividing by 3 on both sides through the multiplication principle with $c = \frac{1}{3}$ results in the final answer of $x = \frac{-10}{3}$.

Some equations have a higher degree and are not solved by simply using opposite operations. When an equation has a degree of 2, completing the square is an option. For example, the quadratic equation $x^2 - 6x + 2 = 0$ can be rewritten by completing the square. The goal of completing the square is to get the equation into the form $(x - p)^2 = q$. Using the example, the constant term 2 first needs to be moved over to the opposite side by subtracting. Then, the square can be completed by adding 9 to both sides, which is the square of half of the coefficient of the middle term $-6x$. The current equation is $x^2 - 6x + 9 = 7$. The left side can be factored into a square of a binomial, resulting in $(x - 3)^2 = 7$. To solve for x, the square root of both sides should be taken, resulting in:

$$(x - 3) = \pm\sqrt{7}$$

$$x = 3 \pm \sqrt{7}$$

Other ways of solving quadratic equations include graphing, factoring, and using the quadratic formula. The equation $y = x^2 - 4x + 3$ can be graphed on the coordinate plane, and the solutions can be observed where it crosses the x-axis. The graph will be a parabola that opens up with two solutions at 1 and 3.

The equation can also be factored to find the solutions. The original equation, $y = x^2 - 4x + 3$ can be factored into $y = (x - 1)(x - 3)$. Setting this equal to zero, the x-values are found to be 1 and 3, just as on the graph. Solving by factoring and graphing are not always possible. The quadratic formula is a method of solving quadratic equations that always results in exact solutions.

The formula is:

$$x = \frac{-b \pm \sqrt{b^2 - 4ac}}{2a}$$

where a, b, and c are the coefficients in the original equation in standard form $y = ax^2 + bx + c$. For this example,

$$x = \frac{4 \pm \sqrt{(-4)^2 - 4(1)(3)}}{2(1)} = \frac{4 \pm \sqrt{16 - 12}}{2} = \frac{4 \pm 2}{2} = 1, 3$$

The expression underneath the radical is called the *discriminant*. Without working out the entire formula, the value of the discriminant can reveal the nature of the solutions. If the value of the discriminant $b^2 - 4ac$ is positive, then there will be two real solutions. If the value is zero, there will be one real solution. If the value is negative, the two solutions will be imaginary or complex. If the solutions are complex, it means that the parabola never touches the x-axis. An example of a complex solution can be found by solving the following quadratic: $y = x^2 - 4x + 8$. By using the quadratic formula, the solutions are found to be:

$$x = \frac{4 \pm \sqrt{(-4)^2 - 4(1)(8)}}{2(1)} = \frac{4 \pm \sqrt{16 - 32}}{2} = \frac{4 \pm \sqrt{-16}}{2} = 2 \pm 2i$$

The solutions both have a real part, 2, and an imaginary part, $2i$.

Solving Quadratic Equations in One Variable

Solving quadratic equations is a little trickier. If they take the form $ax^2 - b = 0$, then the equation can be solved by adding b to both sides and dividing by a to get $x^2 = \frac{b}{a}$.

Using the sixth rule above, the solution is $x = \pm\sqrt{\frac{b}{a}}$. Note that this is actually two separate solutions, unless b happens to be zero.

If a quadratic equation has no constant—so that it takes the form $ax^2 + bx = 0$—then the x can be factored out to get $x(ax + b) = 0$. Then, the solutions are $x = 0$, together with the solutions to $ax + b = 0$. Both factors x and $(ax + b)$ can be set equal to zero to solve for x because one of those values must be zero for their product to equal zero. For an equation $ab = 0$ to be true, either $a = 0$, or $b = 0$.

A given quadratic equation $x^2 + bx + c$ can be factored into $(x + A)(x + B)$, where $A + B = b$, and $AB = c$. Finding the values of A and B can take time, but such a pair of numbers can be found by guessing and checking. Looking at the positive and negative factors for c offers a good starting point.

For example, in $x^2 - 5x + 6$, the factors of 6 are 1, 2, and 3. Now, $(-2)(-3) = 6$, and $-2 - 3 = -5$. In general, however, this may not work, in which case another approach may need to be used.

A quadratic equation of the form $x^2 + 2xb + b^2 = 0$ can be factored into $(x + b)^2 = 0$. Similarly, $x^2 - 2xy + y^2 = 0$ factors into $(x - y)^2 = 0$.

In general, the constant term may not be the right value to be factored this way. A more general method for solving these quadratic equations must then be found. The following two methods will work in any situation.

Completing the Square

The first method is called *completing the square*. The idea here is that in any equation $x^2 + 2xb + c = 0$, something could be added to both sides of the equation to get the left side to look like $x^2 + 2xb + b^2$, meaning it could be factored into $(x + b)^2 = 0$.

<u>Example</u>
$x^2 + 6x - 1 = 0$

The left-hand side could be factored if the constant were equal to 9, since $x^2 + 6x + 9 = (x + 3)^2$.

To get a constant of 9 on the left, 10 needs to be added to both sides.

That changes the equation to $x^2 + 6x + 9 = 10$.

Factoring the left gives $(x + 3)^2 = 10$.

Then, the square root of both sides can be taken (remembering that this introduces a $\pm$): $x + 3 = \pm\sqrt{10}$.

Finally, 3 is subtracted from both sides to get two solutions: $x = -3 \pm \sqrt{10}$.

The Quadratic Formula

The first method of completing the square can be used in finding the second method, the quadratic formula. It can be used to solve any quadratic equation. This formula may be the longest method for solving quadratic equations and is commonly used as a last resort after other methods are ruled out.

It can be helpful in memorizing the formula to see where it comes from, so here are the steps involved.

The most general form for a quadratic equation is $ax^2 + bx + c = 0$.

First, dividing both sides by a leaves us with $x^2 + \frac{b}{a}x + \frac{c}{a} = 0$.

To complete the square on the left-hand side, $\frac{c}{a}$ can be subtracted on both sides to get $x^2 + \frac{b}{a}x = -\frac{c}{a}$.

$(\frac{b}{2a})^2$ is then added to both sides.

This gives $x^2 + \frac{b}{a}x + (\frac{b}{2a})^2 = (\frac{b}{2a})^2 - \frac{c}{a}$.

The left can now be factored and the right-hand side simplified to give $(x + \frac{b}{2a})^2 = \frac{b^2 - 4ac}{4a}$.

Taking the square roots gives $x + \frac{b}{2a} = \pm \frac{\sqrt{b^2 - 4ac}}{2a}$.

Solving for x yields the quadratic formula: $x = \frac{-b \pm \sqrt{b^2 - 4ac}}{2a}$.

It isn't necessary to remember how to get this formula, but memorizing the formula itself is the goal.

If an equation involves taking a root, then the first step is to move the root to one side of the equation and everything else to the other side. That way, both sides can be raised to the index of the radical in order to remove it, and solving the equation can continue.

Solving Simple Rational and Radical Equations in One Variable

A *rational expression* is an expression that has the form $\frac{p(x)}{q(x)}$, where $p(x)$ and $q(x)$ are both polynomials. To solve equations or inequalities involving rational expressions, one typically rewrites the expression to get rid of the denominator; as a result, the problem becomes an equation or inequality involving polynomials. One can then apply the techniques mentioned above to complete the solution.

For example, consider the problem $\frac{3x+2}{x-4} = 2$. One can start by multiplying both sides of the equation by $x - 4$. This results in the equation $3x + 2 = 2x - 8$. Now this equation can be solved like any other linear equation. Subtracting $2x$ from both sides and subtracting 2 from both sides gives the solution $x = -10$.

When an equation or an inequality involves radicals, all the radicals must be moved to one side. Then, one can raise both sides to the appropriate power to get rid of the radicals. Remember that the quantity inside a square root must be non-negative. When dealing with inequalities, remember that multiplying both sides by a negative quantity reverses the direction of the inequality.

For example, $\sqrt{x + 1} - 2 = 2$. The first step is to isolate the radical, so add 2 to both sides. This addition results in $\sqrt{x + 1} = 4$. Square both sides, and the result is $x + 1 = 16$, or $x = 15$.

When dealing with multiple radicals, proceed by first isolating one radical, squaring both sides to remove it, and then repeating this process to remove the remaining radicals. Consider the equation $\sqrt{3x - 1} + 1 = \sqrt{x + 1} + 2$. Start by subtracting 1 from both sides, isolating the radical on the left, which results in $\sqrt{3x - 1} = \sqrt{x + 1} + 1$. Now square both sides: $3x - 1 = (\sqrt{x + 1} + 1)^2 = x + 1 + 2\sqrt{x + 1} + 1$, or $3x - 1 = x + 2\sqrt{x + 1} + 2$. Isolate the radical on the right: $2x - 3 = 2\sqrt{x + 1}$. Now square both sides, which results in $4x^2 - 12x + 9 = 4x + 4$. This problem can now be solved by using the quadratic formula.

Solving Systems of Equations

A *system of equations* is a group of equations that have the same variables or unknowns. These equations can be linear, but they are not always so. Finding a solution to a system of equations means finding the values of the variables that satisfy each equation. For a linear system of two equations and two variables, there could be a single solution, no solution, or infinitely many solutions.

A single solution occurs when there is one value for x and y that satisfies the system. This is shown on the graph where the lines cross at exactly one point. When there is no solution, the lines are parallel and do not ever cross. With infinitely many solutions, the equations may look different, but they are the same line. One equation will be a multiple of the other, and on the graph, they lie on top of each other. These three types of systems of linear equations are shown below:

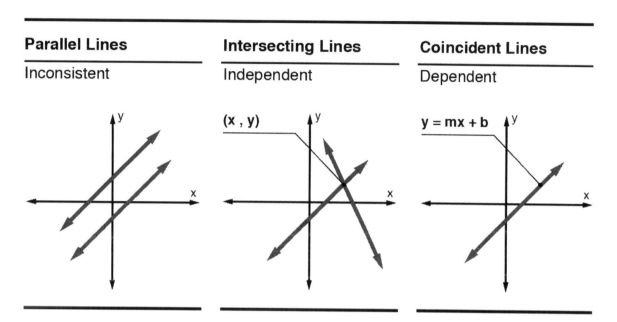

Parallel Lines	Intersecting Lines	Coincident Lines
Inconsistent	Independent	Dependent

The process of elimination can be used to solve a system of equations. For example, the following equations make up a system: $x + 3y = 10$ and $2x - 5y = 9$. Immediately adding these equations does not eliminate a variable, but it is possible to change the first equation by multiplying the whole equation by -2. This changes the first equation to $-2x - 6y = -20$. The equations can be then added to obtain $-11y = -11$. Solving for y yields $y = 1$. To find the rest of the solution, 1 can be substituted in for y in either original equation to find the value of $x = 7$. The solution to the system is $(7, 1)$ because it makes both equations true, and it is the point in which the lines intersect. If the system is *dependent*—having infinitely many solutions—then both variables will cancel out when the elimination method is used, resulting in an equation that is true for many values of x and y. Since the system is dependent, both equations can be simplified to the same equation, or line.

A system can also be solved using *substitution*. This involves solving one equation for a variable and then plugging that solved equation into the other equation in the system. This equation can be solved for one variable, which can then be plugged in to either original equation and solved for the other variable. For example, $x - y = -2$ and $3x + 2y = 9$ can be solved using substitution. The first equation can be solved for x, where $x = -2 + y$. Then it can be plugged into the other equation, $3(-2 + y) + 2y = 9$. Solving for y yields $-6 + 3y + 2y = 9$, where $y = 3$. If $y = 3$, then $x = 1$. This solution can be checked by plugging in these values for the variables in each equation to see if it makes a true statement.

Finally, a solution to a system of equations can be found graphically. The solution to a linear system is the point or points where the lines cross. The values of x and y represent the coordinates (x, y) where the lines intersect. Using the same system of equation as above, they can be solved for y to put them in slope-intercept form, $y = mx + b$. These equations become $y = x + 4$ and $y = -\frac{3}{2}x + 4.5$. The slope

97

is the coefficient of x, and the y-intercept is the constant value. This system with the solution is shown below:

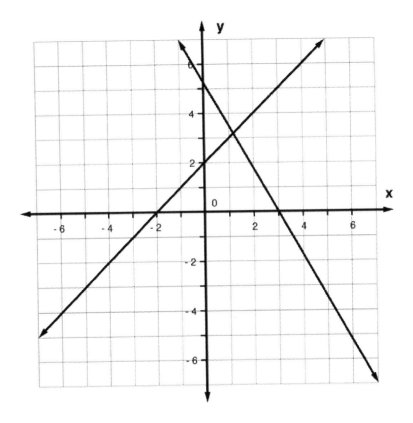

A system of equations may also be made up of a linear and a quadratic equation. These systems may have one solution, two solutions, or no solutions. The graph of these systems involves one straight line and one parabola. Algebraically, these systems can be solved by solving the linear equation for one variable and plugging that answer in to the quadratic equation. If possible, the equation can then be solved to find part of the answer. The graphing method is commonly used for these types of systems. On a graph, these two lines can be found to intersect at one point, at two points across the parabola, or at no points.

Systems with One Linear Equation and One Quadratic Equation

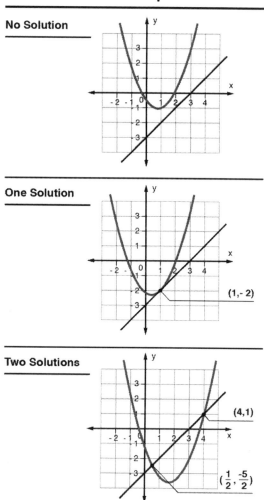

No Solution

One Solution

(1,-2)

Two Solutions

(4,1)

$(\frac{1}{2}, \frac{-5}{2})$

Matrices can also be used to solve systems of linear equations. Specifically, for systems, the coefficients of the linear equations in standard form are the entries in the matrix. Using the same system of linear equations as above, $x - y = -2$ and $3x + 2y = 9$, the matrix to represent the system is $\begin{bmatrix} 1 & -1 \\ 3 & 2 \end{bmatrix}\begin{bmatrix} x \\ y \end{bmatrix} = \begin{bmatrix} -2 \\ 9 \end{bmatrix}$. To solve this system using matrices, the inverse matrix must be found. For a general 2x2 matrix, $\begin{bmatrix} a & b \\ c & d \end{bmatrix}$, the inverse matrix is found by the expression $\frac{1}{ad-bc}\begin{bmatrix} d & -b \\ -c & a \end{bmatrix}$. The inverse matrix for the given system above is $\frac{1}{2--3}\begin{bmatrix} 2 & 1 \\ -3 & 1 \end{bmatrix} = \frac{1}{5}\begin{bmatrix} 2 & 1 \\ -3 & 1 \end{bmatrix}$. The next step in solving is to multiply this identity matrix times the system matrix above. This is given by the following equation: $\frac{1}{5}\begin{bmatrix} 2 & 1 \\ -3 & 1 \end{bmatrix}\begin{bmatrix} 1 & -1 \\ 3 & 2 \end{bmatrix}\begin{bmatrix} x \\ y \end{bmatrix} = \begin{bmatrix} -2 \\ 9 \end{bmatrix}\begin{bmatrix} 2 & 1 \\ -3 & 1 \end{bmatrix}\frac{1}{5}$, which simplifies to $\frac{1}{5}\begin{bmatrix} 5 & 0 \\ 0 & 5 \end{bmatrix}\begin{bmatrix} x \\ y \end{bmatrix} = \frac{1}{5}\begin{bmatrix} 5 \\ 15 \end{bmatrix}$. Solving for the solution matrix, the answer is $\begin{bmatrix} 1 & 0 \\ 0 & 1 \end{bmatrix}\begin{bmatrix} x \\ y \end{bmatrix} = \begin{bmatrix} 1 \\ 3 \end{bmatrix}$. Since the first matrix is the identity matrix, the solution is $x = 1$ and $y = 3$.

Finding solutions to systems of equations is essentially finding what values of the variables make both equations true. It is finding the input value that yields the same output value in both equations. For functions $g(x)$ and $f(x)$, the equation $g(x) = f(x)$ means the output values are being set equal. Solving for the value of x means finding the x-coordinate that gives the same output to both functions. For example, $f(x) = x + 2$ and $g(x) = -3x + 10$ is a system of equations. Setting $f(x) = g(x)$ yields the equation $x + 2 = -3x + 10$. Solving for x gives the x-coordinate $x = -2$ where the two lines cross. This value can also be found by using a table or a graph. On a table, both equations could be given the same inputs, and the outputs could be recorded to find the point(s) where the lines crossed. Any method of solving finds the same solution, but some methods are more appropriate for some systems of equations than others.

Representing and Solving Equations and Inequalities Graphically

Systems of *linear inequalities* are like systems of equations, but the solutions are different. Since inequalities have infinitely many solutions, their systems also have infinitely many solutions. Finding the solutions of inequalities involves graphs. A system of two equations and two inequalities is linear; thus, the lines can be graphed using slope-intercept form. If the inequality has an equals sign, the line is solid. If the inequality only has a greater than or less than symbol, the line on the graph is dotted. Dashed lines indicate that points lying on the line are not included in the solution. After the lines are graphed, a region is shaded on one side of the line. This side is found by determining if a point—known as a *test point*—lying on one side of the line produces a true inequality. If it does, that side of the graph is shaded. If the point produces a false inequality, the line is shaded on the opposite side from the point. The graph of a system of inequalities involves shading the intersection of the two shaded regions. An example of a system of linear inequalities is shown below. The smaller shaded region that overlaps both larger shaded regions is the solution to the system. Any point that lies in this region or on the blue line in that region produces a true inequality for either inequality used.

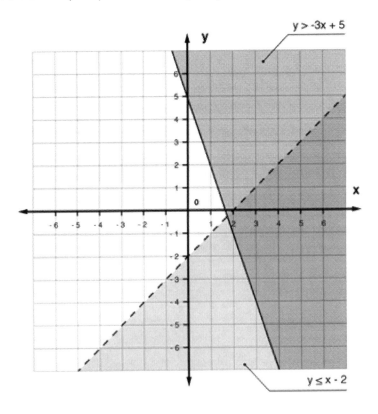

A graph of the solution set for a linear inequality shows the ordered pairs that make the statement true. The graph consists of a boundary line dividing the coordinate plane and shading on one side of the boundary. The boundary line should be graphed just as a linear equation would be graphed (see section on *Understanding Connections Between Algebraic and Graphical Representations*). If the inequality symbol is > or <, a dashed line can be used to indicate that the line is not part of the solution set. If the inequality symbol is ≥ or ≤, a solid line can be used to indicate that the boundary line is included in the solution set. An ordered pair (x, y) on either side of the line should be chosen to test in the inequality statement. If substituting the values for x and y results in a true statement $(15(3) + 25(2) > 90)$, that ordered pair and all others on that side of the boundary line are part of the solution set. To indicate this, that region of the graph should be shaded. If substituting the ordered pair results in a false statement, the ordered pair and all others on that side are not part of the solution set. Therefore, the other region of the graph contains the solutions and should be shaded.

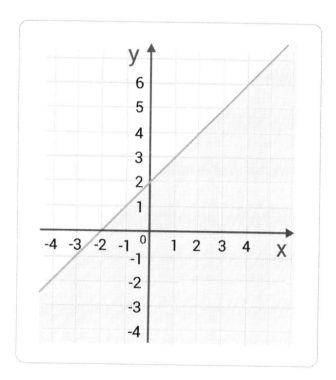

A question may simply ask whether a given ordered pair is a solution to a given inequality. To determine this, the values should be substituted for the ordered pair into the inequality. If the result is a true statement, the ordered pair is a solution; if the result is a false statement, the ordered pair is not a solution.

Creating Equations and Inequalities to Represent Relationships and Using Them to Solve Problems

An algebraic expression is a statement about unknown quantities expressed in mathematical symbols. The statement *five times a number added to forty* is expressed as $5x + 40$. An equation is a statement in which two expressions (with at least one containing a variable) are equal to one another. The statement *five times a number added to forty is equal to ten* is expressed as $5x + 40 = 10$.

Real world scenarios can also be expressed mathematically. Suppose a job pays its employees $300 per week and $40 for each sale made. The weekly pay is represented by the expression $40x + 300$ where x is the number of sales made during the week.

Consider the following scenario: Bob had $20 and Tom had $4. After selling 4 ice cream cones to Bob, Tom has as much money as Bob. The cost of an ice cream cone is an unknown quantity and can be represented by a variable (x). The amount of money Bob has after his purchase is four times the cost of an ice cream cone subtracted from his original $20 $\rightarrow$ $20 - 4x$. The amount of money Tom has after his sale is four times the cost of an ice cream cone added to his original $4 $\rightarrow$ $4x + 4$. After the sale, the amount of money that Bob and Tom have are equal $\rightarrow$ $20 - 4x = 4x + 4$.

When expressing a verbal or written statement mathematically, it is vital to understand words or phrases that can be represented with symbols. The following are examples:

Symbol	Phrase
+	Added to; increased by; sum of; more than
−	Decreased by; difference between; less than; take away
×	Multiplied by; 3(4,5…) times as large; product of
÷	Divided by; quotient of; half (third, etc.) of
=	Is; the same as; results in; as much as; equal to
x,t,n, etc.	A number; unknown quantity; value of; variable

Use of Formulas

Formulas are mathematical expressions that define the value of one quantity, given the value of one or more different quantities. Formulas look like equations because they contain variables, numbers, operators, and an equal sign. All formulas are equations but not all equations are formulas. A formula must have more than one variable. For example, $2x + 7 = y$ is an equation and a formula (it relates the unknown quantities x and y). However, $2x + 7 = 3$ is an equation but not a formula (it only expresses the value of the unknown quantity x).

Formulas are typically written with one variable alone (or isolated) on one side of the equal sign. This variable can be thought of as the *subject* in that the formula is stating the value of the *subject* in terms of the relationship between the other variables. Consider the distance formula: $distance = rate \times time$ or $d = rt$. The value of the subject variable d (distance) is the product of the variable r and t (rate and time). Given the rate and time, the distance traveled can easily be determined by substituting the values into the formula and evaluating.

The formula $P = 2l + 2w$ expresses how to calculate the perimeter of a rectangle (P) given its length (l) and width (w). To find the perimeter of a rectangle with a length of 3ft and a width of 2ft, these values are substituted into the formula for l and w: $P = 2(3ft) + 2(2ft)$. Following the order of operations, the perimeter is determined to be 10ft. When working with formulas such as these, including units is an important step.

Given a formula expressed in terms of one variable, the formula can be manipulated to express the relationship in terms of any other variable. In other words, the formula can be rearranged to change which variable is the *subject*. To solve for a variable of interest by manipulating a formula, the equation may be solved as if all other variables were numbers. The same steps for solving are followed, leaving operations in terms of the variables instead of calculating numerical values. For the formula $P = 2l + 2w$, the perimeter is the subject expressed in terms of the length and width. To write a formula to calculate the width of a rectangle, given its length and perimeter, the previous formula relating the three variables is solved for the variable w. If P and l were numerical values, this is a two-step linear equation solved by subtraction and division. To solve the equation $P = 2l + 2w$ for w, $2l$ is first subtracted from both sides: $P - 2l = 2w$. Then both sides are divided by 2: $\frac{P-2l}{2} = w$.

Functions and Function Notation, Interpreting Key Features of Graphs and Tables in Terms of Quantities

A relation is a set of input and output values that can be written as ordered pairs. A function is a relation in which each input is paired with exactly one output. The domain of a function consists of all inputs, and the range consists of all outputs. Graphing the ordered pairs of a linear function produces a straight line. An example of a function would be $f(x) = 4x + 4$, read "f of x is equal to four times x plus four." In this example, the input would be x and the output would be f(x). Ordered pairs would be represented as (x, f(x)). To find the output for an input value of 3, 3 would be substituted for x into the function as follows: $f(3) = 4(3) + 4$, resulting in $f(3) = 16$. Therefore, the ordered pair $(3, f(3)) = (3, 16)$. Note f(x) is a function of x denoted by f. Functions of x could be named g(x), read "g of x"; p(x), read "p of x"; etc.

A linear function could also be written in the form of an equation with two variables. Typically, the variable x represents the inputs and the variable y represents the outputs. The variable x is considered the independent variable and y the dependent variable. The above function would be written as $y = 4x + 4$. Ordered pairs are written in the form (x, y).

Domain and Range of a Function

The domain and range of a function can be found visually by its plot on the coordinate plane. In the function $f(x) = x^2 - 3$, for example, the domain is all real numbers because the parabola stretches as far left and as far right as it can go, with no restrictions. This means that any input value from the real number system will yield an answer in the real number system. For the range, the inequality $y \geq -3$ would be used to describe the possible output values because the parabola has a minimum at $y = -3$. This means there will not be any real output values less than -3 because -3 is the lowest value it reaches on the y-axis.

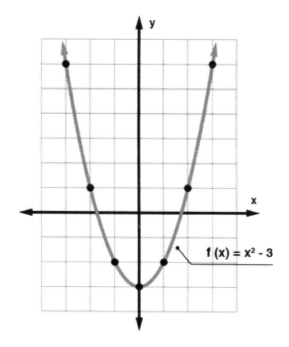

These same answers for domain and range can be found by observing a table. The table below shows that from input values $x = -1$ to $x = 1$, the output results in a minimum of -3. On each side of $x = 0$, the numbers increase, showing that the range is all real numbers greater than or equal to -3.

x (domain/input)	y (range/output)
-2	1
-1	-2
0	-3
-1	-2
2	1

Writing a Function that Describes a Relationship Between Two Quantities and Using Them to Model Situations, and Translating Between the Two Forms

A *function* is defined as a relationship between inputs and outputs where there is only one output value for a given input. As an example, the following function is in function notation: $f(x) = 3x - 4$. The $f(x)$ represents the output value for an input of x. If $x = 2$, the equation becomes:

$$f(2) = 3(2) - 4 = 6 - 4 = 2$$

The input of 2 yields an output of 2, forming the ordered pair $(2, 2)$. The following set of ordered pairs corresponds to the given function: $(2, 2), (0, -4), (-2, -10)$. The set of all possible inputs of a function is its *domain*, and all possible outputs is called the *range*. By definition, each member of the domain is paired with only one member of the range.

Functions can also be defined recursively. In this form, they are not defined explicitly in terms of variables. Instead, they are defined using previously-evaluated function outputs, starting with either $f(0)$ or $f(1)$. An example of a recursively-defined function is:

$$f(1) = 2, f(n) = 2f(n-1) + 2n, n > 1$$

The domain of this function is the set of all integers.

Different types of functions behave in different ways. The quadratic function described above can be described as decreasing from left to right until the input value of zero, then increasing after that. A function is defined to be increasing over a subset of its domain if for all $x_1 \geq x_2$ in that interval, $f(x_1) \geq f(x_2)$. Also, a function is decreasing over an interval if for all $x_1 \geq x_2$ in that interval, $f(x_1) \leq f(x_2)$. A point in which a function changes from increasing to decreasing can also be labeled as the *maximum value* of a function if it is the largest point the graph reaches on the y-axis. A point in which a function changes from decreasing to increasing can be labeled as the minimum value of a function if it is the smallest point the graph reaches on the y-axis. Maximum values are also known as *extreme values*. The graph of a continuous function does not have any breaks or jumps in the graph. This description is not true of all functions. A radical function, for example, $f(x) = \sqrt{x}$, has a restriction for the domain and range because there are no real negative inputs or outputs for this function. The domain can be stated as $x \geq 0$, and the range is $y \geq 0$.

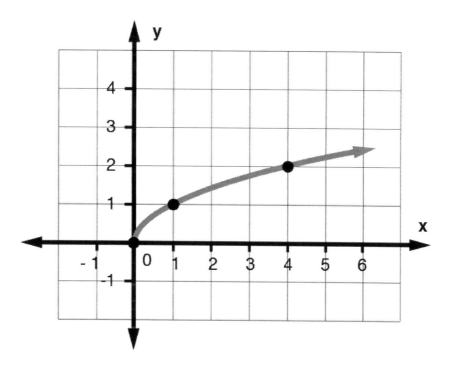

A piecewise-defined function also has a different appearance on the graph. In the following function, there are three equations defined over different intervals. It is a function because there is only one y-value for each x-value, passing the Vertical Line Test. The domain is all real numbers less than or equal to 6. The range is all real numbers greater than zero. From left to right, the graph decreases to zero, then increases to almost 4, and then jumps to 6.

From input values greater than 2, the input decreases just below 8 to 4, and then stops.

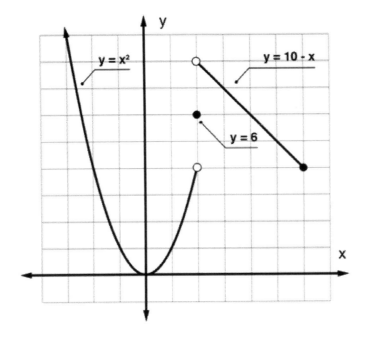

Logarithmic and exponential functions also have different behavior than other functions. These two types of functions are inverses of each other. The *inverse* of a function can be found by switching the place of x and y, and solving for y. When this is done for the exponential equation, $y = 2^x$, the function $y = \log_2 x$ is found. The general form of a *logarithmic function* is $y = \log_b x$, which says b raised to the y power equals x.

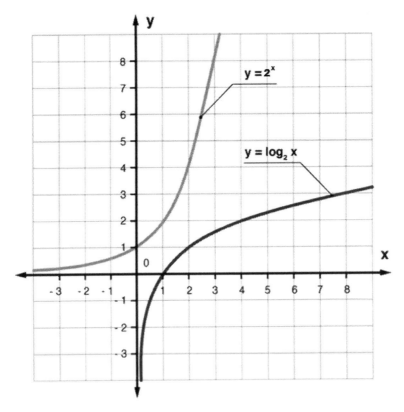

The thick black line on the graph above represents the logarithmic function $y = \log_2 x$. This curve passes through the point $(1, 0)$, just as all log functions do, because any value $b^0 = 1$. The graph of this logarithmic function starts very close to zero, but does not touch the y-axis. The output value will never be zero by the definition of logarithms. The thinner gray line seen above represents the exponential function $y = 2^x$. The behavior of this function is opposite the logarithmic function because the graph of an inverse function is the graph of the original function flipped over the line $y = x$. The curve passes through the point $(0, 1)$ because any number raised to the zero power is one. This curve also gets very close to the x-axis but never touches it because an exponential expression never has an output of zero. The x-axis on this graph is called a horizontal asymptote. An *asymptote* is a line that represents a boundary for a function. It shows a value that the function will get close to, but never reach.

Functions can also be described as being even, odd, or neither. If $f(-x) = f(x)$, the function is even. For example, the function $f(x) = x^2 - 2$ is even. Plugging in $x = 2$ yields an output of $y = 2$. After changing the input to $x = -2$, the output is still $y = 2$. The output is the same for opposite inputs. Another way to observe an even function is by the symmetry of the graph. If the graph is symmetrical about the axis, then the function is even. If the graph is symmetric about the origin, then the function is odd. Algebraically, if $f(-x) = -f(x)$, the function is odd.

Finally, a function can be described as *periodic* if it repeats itself in regular intervals. Common periodic functions are trigonometric functions. For example, $y = \sin x$ is a periodic function with period 2π because it repeats itself every 2π units along the x-axis.

Functions can be built out of the context of a situation. For example, the relationship between the money paid for a gym membership and the months that someone has been a member can be described through a function. If the one-time membership fee is $40 and the monthly fee is $30, then the function can be written $f(x) = 30x + 40$. The x-value represents the number of months the person has been part of the gym, while the output is the total money paid for the membership. The table below shows this relationship. It is a representation of the function because the initial cost is $40 and the cost increases each month by $30.

x (months)	y (money paid to gym)
0	40
1	70
2	100
3	130

Functions can also be built from existing functions. For example, a given function $f(x)$ can be transformed by adding a constant, multiplying by a constant, or changing the input value by a constant. The new function $g(x) = f(x) + k$ represents a vertical shift of the original function. In $f(x) = 3x - 2$, a vertical shift 4 units up would be:

$$g(x) = 3x - 2 + 4 = 3x + 2$$

Multiplying the function times a constant k represents a vertical stretch, based on whether the constant is greater than or less than 1. The function

$$g(x) = kf(x) = 4(3x - 2) = 12x - 8$$

represents a stretch.

Changing the input x by a constant forms the function:

$$g(x) = f(x + k) = 3(x + 4) - 2 = 3x + 12 - 2 = 3x + 10$$

and this represents a horizontal shift to the left 4 units. If $(x - 4)$ was plugged into the function, it would represent a vertical shift.

A composition function can also be formed by plugging one function into another. In function notation, this is written:

$$(f \circ g)(x) = f(g(x))$$

For two functions $f(x) = x^2$ and $g(x) = x - 3$, the composition function becomes:

$$f(g(x)) = (x - 3)^2 = x^2 - 6x + 9$$

The composition of functions can also be used to verify if two functions are inverses of each other. Given the two functions $f(x) = 2x + 5$ and $g(x) = \frac{x-5}{2}$, the composition function can be found $(f \circ g)(x)$. Solving this equation yields:

$$f(g(x)) = 2\left(\frac{x - 5}{2}\right) + 5 = x - 5 + 5 = x$$

It also is true that $g(f(x)) = x$. Since the composition of these two functions gives a simplified answer of x, this verifies that $f(x)$ and $g(x)$ are inverse functions. The domain of $f(g(x))$ is the set of all x-values in the domain of $g(x)$ such that $g(x)$ is in the domain of $f(x)$. Basically, both $f(g(x))$ and $g(x)$ have to be defined.

To build an inverse of a function, $f(x)$ needs to be replaced with y, and the x and y values need to be switched. Then, the equation can be solved for y. For example, given the equation $y = e^{2x}$, the inverse can be found by rewriting the equation $x = e^{2y}$. The natural logarithm of both sides is taken down, and the exponent is brought down to form the equation:

$$\ln(x) = \ln(e)\, 2y$$

$\ln(e)=1$, which yields the equation $\ln(x) = 2y$. Dividing both sides by 2 yields the inverse equation

$$\frac{\ln(x)}{2} = y = f^{-1}(x)$$

The domain of an inverse function is the range of the original function, and the range of an inverse function is the domain of the original function. Therefore, an ordered pair (x, y) on either a graph or a table corresponding to $f(x)$ means that the ordered pair (y, x) exists on the graph of $f^{-1}(x)$. Basically, if $f(x) = y$, then $f^{-1}(y) = x$. For a function to have an inverse, it must be one-to-one. That means it must pass the *Horizontal Line Test*, and if any horizontal line passes through the graph of the function twice, a function is not one-to-one. The domain of a function that is not one-to-one can be restricted to an interval in which the function is one-to-one, to be able to define an inverse function.

Functions can also be formed from combinations of existing functions.

Given $f(x)$ and $g(x)$, the following can be built:

$$f + g$$

$$f - g$$

$$fg$$

$$\frac{f}{g}$$

The domains of $f + g$, $f - g$, and fg are the intersection of the domains of f and g. The domain of $\frac{f}{g}$ is the same set, excluding those values that make $g(x) = 0$.

For example, if:

$$f(x) = 2x + 3$$

$$g(x) = x + 1$$

then

$$\frac{f}{g} = \frac{2x + 3}{x + 1}$$

Its domain is all real numbers except -1.

Common Functions

Three common functions used to model different relationships between quantities are linear, quadratic, and exponential functions. Linear functions are the simplest of the three, and the independent variable x has an exponent of 1. Written in the most common form, $y = mx + b$, the coefficient of x tells how fast the function grows at a constant rate, and the b-value tells the starting point. A quadratic function has an exponent of 2 on the independent variable x. Standard form for this type of function is $y = ax^2 + bx + c$, and the graph is a parabola. These type functions grow at a changing rate. An exponential function has an independent variable in the exponent $y = ab^x$. The graph of these types of functions is described as *growth* or *decay*, based on whether the base, b, is greater than or less than 1. These functions are different from quadratic functions because the base stays constant. A common base is base e.

The following three functions model a linear, quadratic, and exponential function respectively: $y = 2x$, $y = x^2$, and $y = 2^x$. Their graphs are shown below. The first graph, modeling the linear function, shows that the growth is constant over each interval. With a horizontal change of 1, the vertical change is 2. It models a constant positive growth. The second graph shows the quadratic function, which is a curve that is symmetric across the y-axis. The growth is not constant, but the change is mirrored over the axis. The last graph models the exponential function, where the horizontal change of 1 yields a vertical change that increases more and more. The exponential graph gets very close to the x-axis, but never touches it, meaning there is an asymptote there. The y-value can never be zero because the base of 2 can never be raised to an input value that yields an output of zero.

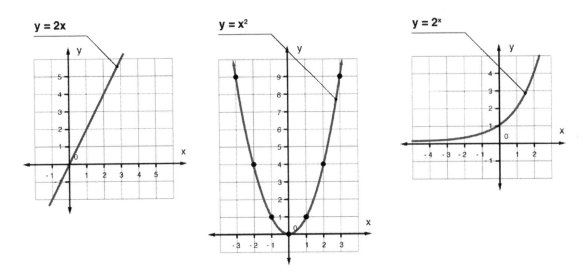

The three tables below show specific values for three types of functions. The third column in each table shows the change in the y-values for each interval. The first table shows a constant change of 2 for each equal interval, which matches the slope in the equation $y = 2x$. The second table shows an increasing change, but it also has a pattern. The increase is changing by 2 more each time, so the change is quadratic. The third table shows the change as factors of the base, 2. It shows a continuing pattern of factors of the base.

y = 2x		
x	y	Δy
1	2	
2	4	2
3	6	2
4	8	2
5	10	2

y = x²		
x	y	Δy
1	1	
2	4	3
3	9	5
4	16	7
5	25	9

y = 2ˣ		
x	y	Δy
1	2	
2	4	2
3	8	4
4	16	8
5	32	16

Given a table of values, the type of function can be determined by observing the change in y over equal intervals. For example, the tables below model two functions. The changes in interval for the x-values is 1 for both tables. For the first table, the y-values increase by 5 for each interval. Since the change is constant, the situation can be described as a linear function. The equation would be $y = 5x + 3$. For the second table, the change for y is 5, 20, 100, and 500, respectively. The increases are multiples of 5,

110

meaning the situation can be modeled by an exponential function. The equation $y = 5^x + 3$ models this situation.

x	y
0	3
1	8
2	13
3	18
4	23

x	y
0	3
1	8
2	28
3	128
4	628

Quadratic equations can be used to model real-world area problems. For example, a farmer may have a rectangular field that he needs to sow with seed. The field has length $x + 8$ and width $2x$. The formula for area should be used: $A = lw$. Therefore:

$$A = (x + 8) \times 2x = 2x^2 + 16x$$

The possible values for the length and width can be shown in a table, with input x and output A. If the equation was graphed, the possible area values can be seen on the y-axis for given x-values.

Exponential growth and decay can be found in real-world situations. For example, if a piece of notebook paper is folded 25 times, the thickness of the paper can be found. To model this situation, a table can be used. The initial point is one-fold, which yields a thickness of 2 papers. For the second fold, the thickness is 4. Since the thickness doubles each time, the table below shows the thickness for the next few folds. Notice the thickness changes by the same factor each time. Since this change for a constant interval of folds is a factor of 2, the function is exponential. The equation for this is $y = 2^x$. For twenty-five folds, the thickness would be 33,554,432 papers.

x (folds)	y (paper thickness)
0	1
1	2
2	4
3	8
4	16
5	32

One exponential formula that is commonly used is the *interest formula*: $A = Pe^{rt}$. In this formula, interest is compounded continuously. A is the value of the investment after the time, t, in years. P is the initial amount of the investment, r is the interest rate, and e is the constant equal to approximately 2.718. Given an initial amount of $200 and a time of 3 years, if interest is compounded continuously at a rate of 6%, the total investment value can be found by plugging each value into the formula. The invested value at the end is $239.44. In more complex problems, the final investment may be given, and the rate may be the unknown. In this case, the formula becomes $239.44 = 200e^{r3}$. Solving for r requires isolating the exponential expression on one side by dividing by 200, yielding the equation

$1.20 = e^{r3}$. Taking the natural log of both sides results in $\ln(1.2) = r3$. Using a calculator to evaluate the logarithmic expression, $r = 0.06 = 6\%$.

When working with logarithms and exponential expressions, it is important to remember the relationship between the two. In general, the logarithmic form is $y = log_b x$ for an exponential form $b^y = x$. Logarithms and exponential functions are inverses of each other.

Identifying zeros of polynomials when suitable factorizations are available, and using the zeros to construct a rough graph of the function defined by the polynomial

Finding the zeros of polynomial functions is the same process as finding the solutions of polynomial equations. These are the points at which the graph of the function crosses the x-axis. As stated previously, factors can be used to find the zeros of a polynomial function. The degree of the function shows the number of possible zeros. If the highest exponent on the independent variable is 4, then the degree is 4, and the number of possible zeros is 4. If there are complex solutions, the number of roots is less than the degree.

Given the function $y = x^2 + 7x + 6$, y can be set equal to zero, and the polynomial can be factored. The equation turns into $0 = (x + 1)(x + 6)$, where $x = -1$ and $x = -6$ are the zeros. Since this is a quadratic equation, the shape of the graph will be a parabola. Knowing that zeros represent the points where the parabola crosses the x-axis, the maximum or minimum point is the only other piece needed to sketch a rough graph of the function. By looking at the function in standard form, the coefficient of x is positive; therefore, the parabola opens *up*. Using the zeros and the minimum, the following rough sketch of the graph can be constructed:

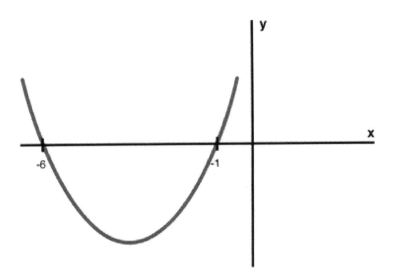

Steps in Solving a Simple Equation

All equations, from the simple to more complex, involve a series of steps that build upon the solution found in the prior step. Sometimes, subsequent steps further manipulate the equation or apply an additional formula, while other times, steps simplify the solution obtained in the prior step or convert its units or presentation in one way or another. In the latter cases, solutions to the two steps are actually equivalent, but presented in different forms. In all situations, it is important to understand and be able to logically explain the reason behind each step involved in finding a solution to a given problem and why the given procedure was followed. To that end, one should verify that his or her obtained answer is reasonable for the provided problem and can defend its accuracy.

For example, when solving a linear equation, the desired result requires determining a numerical value for the unknown variable. If given a linear equation involving addition, subtraction, multiplication, or division, working backwards isolates the variable. Addition and subtraction are inverse operations, as are multiplication and division. Therefore, they can be used to cancel each other out.

The first steps to solving linear equations are distributing, if necessary, and combining any like terms on the same side of the equation. Sides of an equation are separated by an *equal* sign. Next, the equation is manipulated to show the variable on one side. Whatever is done to one side of the equation must be done to the other side of the equation to remain equal. Inverse operations are then used to isolate the variable and undo the order of operations backwards. Addition and subtraction are undone, then multiplication and division are undone.

For example, solve $4(t - 2) + 2t - 4 = 2(9 - 2t)$

Distributing: $4t - 8 + 2t - 4 = 18 - 4t$

Combining like terms: $6t - 12 = 18 - 4t$

Adding $4t$ to each side to move the variable: $10t - 12 = 18$

Adding 12 to each side to isolate the variable: $10t = 30$

Dividing each side by 10 to isolate the variable: $t = 3$

The answer can be checked by substituting the value for the variable into the original equation, ensuring that both sides calculate to be equal.

Calculating and Interpreting the Average Rate of Change of a Function (Presented Symbolically or as a Table) Over a Specified Interval and Estimating Rate of Change From Graph

Rate of change for any line calculates the steepness of the line over a given interval. Rate of change is also known as the slope or rise/run. The rates of change for nonlinear functions vary depending on the interval being used for the function. The rate of change over one interval may be zero, while the next interval may have a positive rate of change. The equation plotted on the graph below, $y = x^2$, is a quadratic function and non-linear. The average rate of change from points $(0, 0)$ to $(1, 1)$ is 1 because the vertical change is 1 over the horizontal change of 1. For the next interval, $(1, 1)$ to $(2, 4)$, the average rate of change is 3 because the slope is $\frac{3}{1}$.

You can see that here:

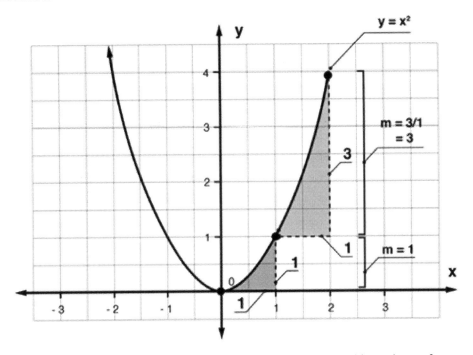

The rate of change for a linear function is constant and can be determined based on a few representations. One method is to place the equation in slope-intercept form: $y = mx + b$. Thus, m is the slope, and b is the y-intercept. In the graph below, the equation is $y = x + 1$, where the slope is 1 and the y-intercept is 1. For every vertical change of 1 unit, there is a horizontal change of 1 unit. The x-intercept is -1, which is the point where the line crosses the x-axis.

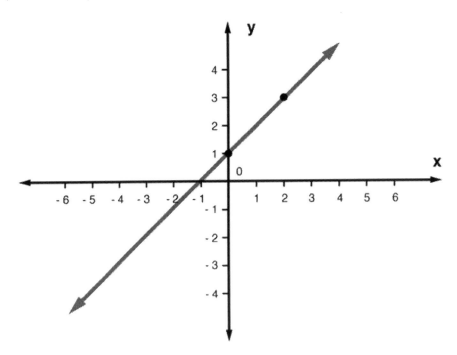

Probability and Statistics

Summarizing and Interpreting Data, Making Predictions and Solving Problems Based on the Data, and Recognizing Possible Associations and Trends in the Data

Representing Data

Most statistics involve collecting a large amount of data, analyzing it, and then making decisions based on previously known information. These decisions also can be measured through additional data collection and then analyzed. Therefore, the cycle can repeat itself over and over. Representing the data visually is a large part of the process, and many plots on the real number line exist that allow this to be done. For example, a *dot plot* uses dots to represent data points above the number line. Also, a *histogram* represents a data set as a collection of rectangles, which illustrate the frequency distribution of the data. Finally, a *box plot* (also known as a *box and whisker plot*) plots a data set on the number line by segmenting the distribution into four quartiles that are divided equally in half by the median. Here's an example of a box plot, a histogram, and a dot plot for the same data set:

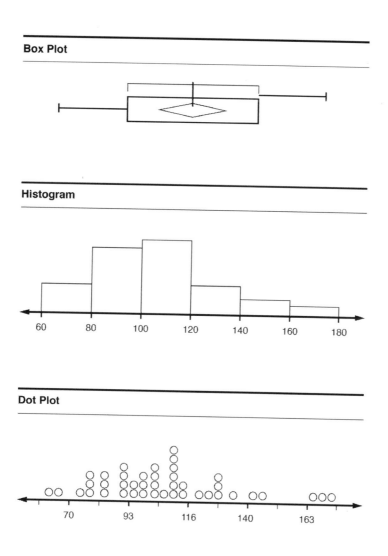

Comparing Data

Comparing data sets within statistics can mean many things. The first way to compare data sets is by looking at the center and spread of each set. The center of a data set can mean two things: median or mean. The *median* is the value that's halfway into each data set, and it splits the data into two intervals. The *mean* is the average value of the data within a set. It's calculated by adding up all of the data in the set and dividing the total by the number of data points. Outliers can significantly impact the mean. Additionally, two completely different data sets can have the same mean. For example, a data set with values ranging from zero to 100 and a data set with values ranging from 44 to 56 can both have means of 50. The first data set has a much wider range, which is known as the *spread* of the data. This measures how varied the data is within each set. Spread can be defined further as either interquartile range or standard deviation. The *interquartile range (IQR)* is the range of the middle 50 percent of the data set. This range can be seen in the large rectangle on a box plot. The *standard deviation (σ)* quantifies the amount of variation with respect to the mean. A lower standard deviation shows that the data set doesn't differ greatly from the mean. A larger standard deviation shows that the data set is spread out farther from the mean. The formula for standard deviation is:

$$\sigma = \sqrt{\frac{\sum (x - \bar{x})^2}{n - 1}}$$

x is each value in the data set, $\bar{x}$ is the mean, and n is the total number of data points in the set.

Interpreting Data

The shape of a data set is another way to compare two or more sets of data. If a data set isn't symmetric around its mean, it's said to be *skewed*. If the tail to the left of the mean is longer, it's said to be *skewed to the left*. In this case, the mean is less than the median. Conversely, if the tail to the right of the mean is longer, it's said to be *skewed to the right* and the mean is greater than the median. When classifying a data set according to its shape, its overall *skewness* is being discussed. If the mean and median are equal, the data set isn't skewed; it is *symmetric*.

An *outlier* is a data point that lies a great distance away from the majority of the data set. It also can be labelled as an *extreme value*. Technically, an outlier is any value that falls 1.5 times the IQR above the upper quartile or 1.5 times the IQR below the lower quartile. The effect of outliers in the data set is seen visually because they affect the mean. If there's a large difference between the mean and mode, outliers are the cause. The mean shows bias towards the outlying values. However, the median won't be affected as greatly by outliers.

Linear Regression

Regression lines are a way to calculate a relationship between the independent variable and the dependent variable. A straight line means that there's a linear trend in the data. The average daily temperature example above is one in which a straight line represents the data because the shape of the scatterplot resembles a straight line. Technology can be used to find the equation of this line (e.g., a graphing calculator or Microsoft Excel®). In either case, all of the data points are entered and a line is "fit" that best represents the shape of the data. Other functions used to model data sets include quadratic and exponential models. Here's an example of a data set and its regression line:

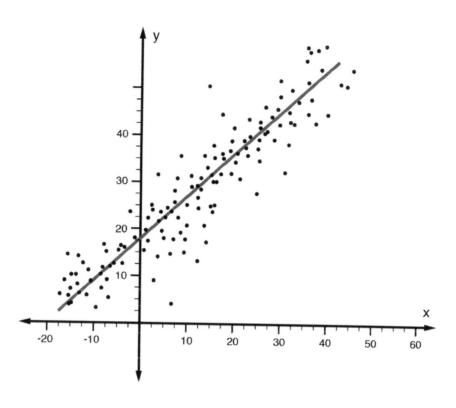

Estimating Data Points

Regression lines can be used to estimate data points not already given. For example, if an equation of a line is found that fit the temperature and beach visitor data set, its input is the average daily temperature and its output is the projected number of visitors. Thus, the number of beach visitors on a 100-degree day can be estimated. The output is a data point on the regression line, and the number of daily visitors is expected to be greater than on a 96-degree day because the regression line has a positive slope.

Interpreting the Regression Line

The formula for a regression line is $y = mx + b$, where m is the slope and b is the y-intercept. Both the slope and y-intercept are found in the *Method of Least Squares*, which is the process of finding the equation of the line through minimizing residuals. The slope represents the rate of change in y as x gets larger. Therefore, because y is the dependent variable, the slope actually provides the predicted values given the independent variable. The y-intercept is the predicted value for when the independent variable equals zero. In the temperature example, the y-intercept is the expected number of beach visitors for a very cold average daily temperature of zero degrees.

Probabilities of Single and Compound Events

A *simple event* consists of only one outcome. The most popular simple event is flipping a coin, which results in either heads or tails. A *compound event* results in more than one outcome and consists of more than one simple event. An example of a compound event is flipping a coin while tossing a die. The result is either heads or tails on the coin and a number from one to six on the die. The probability of a simple event is calculated by dividing the number of possible outcomes by the total number of outcomes. Therefore, the probability of obtaining heads on a coin is $\frac{1}{2}$, and the probability of rolling a 6 on a die is $\frac{1}{6}$. The probability of compound events is calculated using the basic idea of the probability of simple events. If the two events are independent, the probability of one outcome is equal to the product of the probabilities of each simple event. For example, the probability of obtaining heads on a coin and rolling a 6 is equal to $\frac{1}{2} \times \frac{1}{6} = \frac{1}{12}$. The probability of either A or B occurring is equal to the sum of the probabilities minus the probability that both A and B will occur. Therefore, the probability of obtaining either heads on a coin or rolling a 6 on a die is:

$$\frac{1}{2} + \frac{1}{6} - \frac{1}{12} = \frac{7}{12}$$

The two events aren't mutually exclusive because they can happen at the same time. If two events are mutually exclusive, and the probability of both events occurring at the same time is zero, the probability of event A or B occurring equals the sum of both probabilities. An example of calculating the probability of two mutually exclusive events is determining the probability of pulling a king or a queen from a deck of cards. The two events cannot occur at the same time.

Approximating the Probability of a Chance Event, and Developing a Probability Model and Using it to Find Probabilities of Events

Probability is a measure of how likely an event is to occur. Probability is written as a fraction between zero and one. If an event has a probability of zero, the event will never occur. If an event has a probability of one, the event will definitely occur. If the probability of an event is closer to zero, the event is unlikely to occur. If the probability of an event is closer to one, the event is more likely to occur. For example, a probability of $\frac{1}{2}$ means that the event is equally as likely to occur as it is not to occur. An example of this is tossing a coin. To calculate the probability of an event, the number of favorable outcomes is divided by the number of total outcomes. For example, suppose you have 2 raffle tickets out of 20 total tickets sold. The probability that you win the raffle is calculated:
$\frac{number\ of\ favorable\ outcomes}{total\ number of\ outcomes} = \frac{2}{20} = \frac{1}{10}$ (always reduce fractions). Therefore, the probability of winning the raffle is $\frac{1}{10}$ or 0.1.

Chance is the measure of how likely an event is to occur, written as a percent. If an event will never occur, the event has a 0% chance. If an event will certainly occur, the event has a 100% chance. If an event will sometimes occur, the event has a chance somewhere between 0% and 100%. To calculate chance, probability is calculated and the fraction is converted to a percent.

The probability of multiple events occurring can be determined by multiplying the probability of each event. For example, suppose you flip a coin with heads and tails, and roll a six-sided dice numbered one through six. To find the probability that you will flip heads AND roll a two, the probability of each event is determined and those fractions are multiplied. The probability of flipping heads is $\frac{1}{2} \left(\frac{1\ side\ with\ heads}{2\ sides\ total} \right)$ and the probability of rolling a two is $\frac{1}{6} \left(\frac{1\ side\ with\ a\ 2}{6\ total\ sides} \right)$. The probability of flipping heads AND rolling a 2 is: $\frac{1}{2} \times \frac{1}{6} = \frac{1}{12}$.

The above scenario with flipping a coin and rolling a dice is an example of independent events. Independent events are circumstances in which the outcome of one event does not affect the outcome of the other event. Conversely, dependent events are ones in which the outcome of one event affects the outcome of the second event. Consider the following scenario: a bag contains 5 black marbles and 5 white marbles. What is the probability of picking 2 black marbles without replacing the marble after the first pick?

The probability of picking a black marble on the first pick is $\frac{5}{10}$ $\left(\frac{5\ black\ marbles}{10\ total\ marbles}\right)$. Assuming that a black marble was picked, there are now 4 black marbles and 5 white marbles for the second pick. Therefore, the probability of picking a black marble on the second pick is $\frac{4}{9}$ $\left(\frac{4\ black\ marbles}{9\ total\ marbles}\right)$. To find the probability of picking two black marbles, the probability of each is multiplied: $\frac{5}{10} \times \frac{4}{9} = \frac{20}{90} = \frac{2}{9}$.

Using Measures of Center (Mean) to Draw Inferences About Populations Including Summarizing Numerical Data Sets and Calculation of Measures of Center

The center of the sample set can be represented by its mean, median, or mode. The mean is the average of the data set, calculated by adding the data values and dividing by the sample size. The median is the value of the data point in the middle when the sample is arranged in numerical order. If the sample has an even number of data points, the mean of the two middle values is the median. The mode is the value that appears most often in a data set. It is possible to have multiple modes (if different values repeat equally as often) or no mode (if no value repeats).

Methods for determining the spread of the sample include calculating the range and standard deviation for the data. The range is calculated by subtracting the lowest value from the highest value in the set.

The standard deviation of the sample can be calculated using the formula: $\sigma = \sqrt{\frac{\sum(x-\bar{x})^2}{n-1}}$, where $\bar{x}$ = sample mean and n = sample size.

A *normal distribution* of data follows the shape of a bell curve as shown here:

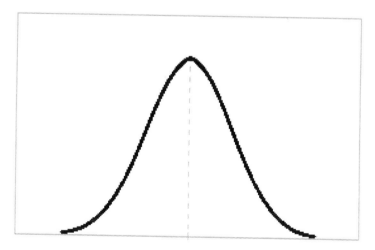

In a normal distribution, the data set's median, mean, and mode are equal. Therefore, 50 percent of its values are less than the mean and 50 percent are greater than the mean. Data sets that follow this shape can be generalized using normal distributions. Normal distributions are described as *frequency distributions* in which the data set is plotted as percentages rather than true data points. A *relative frequency distribution* is one where the y-axis is between zero and 1, which is the same as 0% to 100%. Within a standard deviation, 68 percent of the values are within 1 standard deviation of the mean, 95 percent of the values are within 2 standard deviations of the mean, and 99.7 percent of the values are within 3 standard deviations of the mean. The number of standard deviations that a data point falls from the mean is called the *z-score*. The formula for the z-score is $Z = \frac{x-\mu}{\sigma}$, where μ is the mean, σ is the standard deviation, and x is the data point. This formula is used to fit any data set that resembles a normal distribution to a standard normal distribution, and the process is known as *standardizing*. Here is a normal distribution with labelled z-scores:

Normal Distribution with Labelled Z-Scores

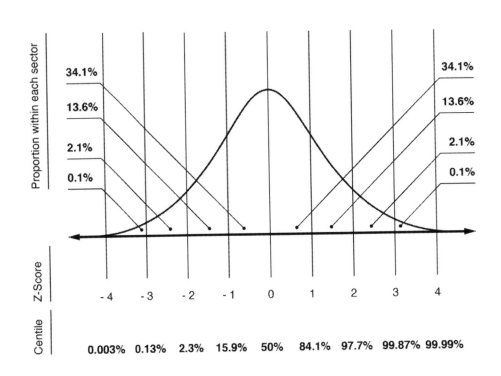

Population percentages can be estimated using normal distributions. For example, the probability that a data point will be less than the mean, or that the z-score will be less than 0, is 50%. Similarly, the probability that a data point will be within 1 standard deviation of the mean, or that the z-score will be between -1 and 1, is about 68.2%. When using a table, the left column states how many standard deviations (to one decimal place) away from the mean the point is, and the row heading states the second decimal place. The entries in the table corresponding to each column and row give the probability, which is equal to the area.

Using Statistics to Gain Information About a Population, Generalizing Information About a Population from a Sample of the Population

Statistics involves making decisions and predictions about larger data sets based on smaller data sets. Basically, the information from one part or subset can help predict what happens in the entire data set or population at large. The entire process involves guessing, and the predictions and decisions may not be 100 percent correct all of the time; however, there is some truth to these predictions, and the decisions do have mathematical support. The smaller data set is called a *sample* and the larger data set (in which the decision is being made) is called a *population*. A *random sample* is used as the sample, which is an unbiased collection of data points that represents the population as well as it can. There are many methods of forming a random sample, and all adhere to the fact that every potential data point has a predetermined probability of being chosen. Statistical inference, based in probability theory, makes calculated assumptions about an entire population based on data from a sample set from that population.

A population is the entire set of people or things of interest. Suppose a study is intended to determine the number of hours of sleep per night for college females in the U.S. The population would consist of EVERY college female in the country. A sample is a subset of the population that may be used for the study. It would not be practical to survey every female college student, so a sample might consist of 100 students per school from 20 different colleges in the country. From the results of the survey, a sample statistic can be calculated. A sample statistic is a numerical characteristic of the sample data, including mean and variance. A sample statistic can be used to estimate a corresponding population parameter. A population parameter is a numerical characteristic of the entire population. Suppose the sample data had a mean (average) of 5.5. This sample statistic can be used as an estimate of the population parameter (average hours of sleep for every college female in the U.S.).

Confidence Intervals

A population parameter is usually unknown and therefore is estimated using a sample statistic. This estimate may be highly accurate or relatively inaccurate based on errors in sampling. A confidence interval indicates a range of values likely to include the true population parameter. These are constructed at a given confidence level, such as 95%. This means that if the same population is sampled repeatedly, the true population parameter would occur within the interval for 95% of the samples.

The accuracy of a population parameter based on a sample statistic may also be affected by measurement error, which is the difference between a quantity's true value and its measured value. Measurement error can be divided into random error and systematic error. An example of random error for the previous scenario would be a student reporting 8 hours of sleep when she actually sleeps 7 hours per night. Systematic errors are those attributed to the measurement system. Suppose the sleep survey gave response options of 2, 4, 6, 8, or 10 hours. This would lead to systematic measurement error.

Geometry and Measurements

Using Congruence and Similarity Criteria for Triangles to Solve Problems and to Prove Relationships in Geometric Figures

To prove theorems about triangles, basic definitions involving triangles (e.g., equilateral, isosceles, etc.) need to be known. Proven theorems concerning lines and angles can be applied to prove theorems about triangles. Common theorems to be proved include: the sum of all angles in a triangle equals 180 degrees; the sum of the lengths of two sides of a triangle is greater than the length of the third side; the base angles of an isosceles triangle are congruent; the line segment connecting the midpoint of two sides of a triangle is parallel to the third side and its length is half the length of the third side; and the medians of a triangle all meet at a single point.

Triangle Congruence

There are five theorems to show that triangles are congruent when it's unknown whether each pair of angles and sides are congruent. Each theorem is a shortcut that involves different combinations of sides and angles that must be true for the two triangles to be congruent. For example, *side-side-side (SSS)* states that if all sides are equal, the triangles are congruent. *Side-angle-side (SAS)* states that if two pairs of sides are equal and the included angles are congruent, then the triangles are congruent. Similarly, *angle-side-angle (ASA)* states that if two pairs of angles are congruent and the included side lengths are equal, the triangles are similar. *Angle-angle-side (AAS)* states that two triangles are congruent if they have two pairs of congruent angles and a pair of corresponding equal side lengths that aren't included. Finally, *hypotenuse-leg (HL)* states that if two right triangles have equal hypotenuses and an equal pair of shorter sides, then the triangles are congruent. An important item to note is that angle-angle-angle *(AAA)* is not enough information to have congruence. It's important to understand why these rules work by using rigid motions to show congruence between the triangles with the given properties. For example, three reflections are needed to show why *SAS* follows from the definition of congruence.

Similarity for Two Triangles

If two angles of one triangle are congruent with two angles of a second triangle, the triangles are similar. This is because, within any triangle, the sum of the angle measurements is 180 degrees. Therefore, if two are congruent, the third angle must also be congruent because their measurements are equal. Three congruent pairs of angles mean that the triangles are similar.

Proving Congruence and Similarity

The criteria needed to prove triangles are congruent involves both angle and side congruence. Both pairs of related angles and sides need to be of the same measurement to use congruence in a proof. The criteria to prove similarity in triangles involves proportionality of side lengths. Angles must be congruent in similar triangles; however, corresponding side lengths only need to be a constant multiple of each other. Once similarity is established, it can be used in proofs as well. Relationships in geometric figures other than triangles can be proven using triangle congruence and similarity. If a similar or congruent triangle can be found within another type of geometric figure, their criteria can be used to prove a relationship about a given formula. For example, a rectangle can be broken up into two congruent triangles.

Properties of Polygons and Circles

A polygon is a closed two-dimensional figure consisting of three or more sides. Polygons can be either convex or concave. A polygon that has interior angles all measuring less than 180° is convex. A concave polygon has one or more interior angles measuring greater than 180°. Examples are shown below.

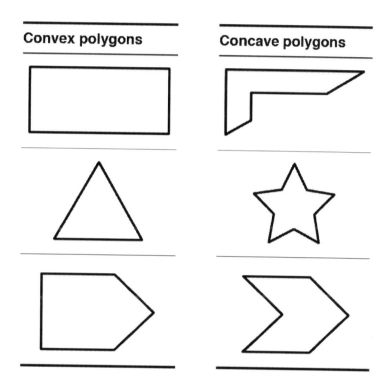

Polygons can be classified by the number of sides (also equal to the number of angles) they have. The following are the names of polygons with a given number of sides or angles:

# of sides	3	4	5	6	7	8	9	10
Name of polygon	Triangle	Quadrilateral	Pentagon	Hexagon	Septagon (or heptagon)	Octagon	Nonagon	Decagon

Equiangular polygons are polygons in which the measure of every interior angle is the same. The sides of equilateral polygons are always the same length. If a polygon is both equiangular and equilateral, the polygon is defined as a regular polygon. Examples are shown below.

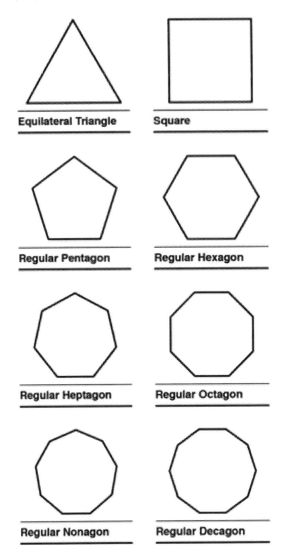

Equilateral Triangle   **Square**

Regular Pentagon   **Regular Hexagon**

Regular Heptagon   **Regular Octagon**

Regular Nonagon   **Regular Decagon**

Triangles can be further classified by their sides and angles. A triangle with its largest angle measuring 90° is a right triangle.

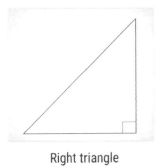

Right triangle

A triangle with the largest angle less than 90° is an acute triangle. A triangle with the largest angle greater than 90° is an obtuse triangle.

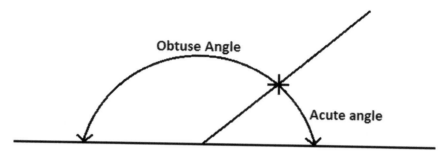

A triangle consisting of two equal sides and two equal angles is an isosceles triangle. A triangle with three equal sides and three equal angles is an equilateral triangle. A triangle with no equal sides or angles is a scalene triangle.

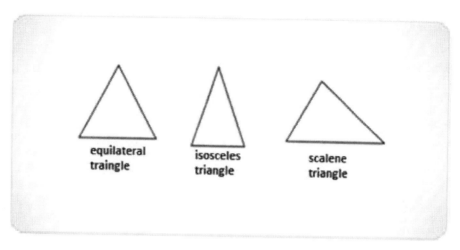

Quadrilaterals can be further classified according to their sides and angles. A quadrilateral with exactly one pair of parallel sides is called a trapezoid. A quadrilateral that shows both pairs of opposite sides parallel is a parallelogram. Parallelograms include rhombuses, rectangles, and squares. A rhombus has four equal sides. A rectangle has four equal angles (90° each). A square has four 90° angles and four equal sides. Therefore, a square is both a rhombus and a rectangle.

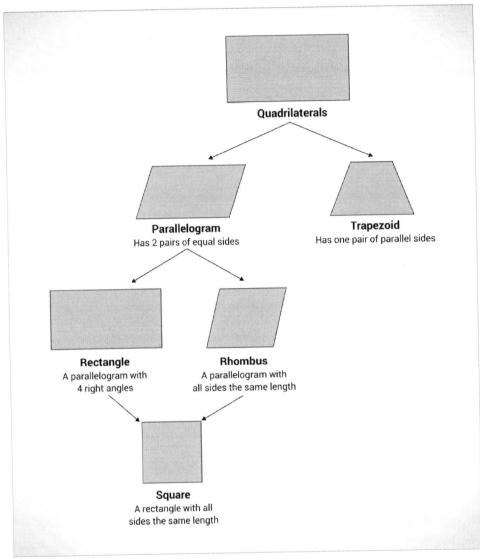

There are many key facts related to geometry that are applicable. The sum of the measures of the angles of a triangle are 180°, and for a quadrilateral, the sum is 360°. Rectangles and squares each have four right angles. A *right angle* has a measure of 90°.

Perimeter

The *perimeter* is the distance around a figure or the sum of all sides of a polygon.

The *formula for the perimeter of a square* is four times the length of a side. For example, the following square has side lengths of 5 meters:

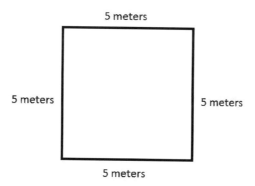

The perimeter is 20 meters because 4 times 5 is 20.

The *formula for a perimeter of a rectangle* is the sum of twice the length and twice the width. For example, if the length of a rectangle is 10 inches and the width 8 inches, then the perimeter is 36 inches because $P = 2l + 2w = 2(10) + 2(8) = 20 + 16 = 36$ inches.

Area

The area is the amount of space inside of a figure, and there are formulas associated with area.

The area of a triangle is the product of ½ the base and height. For example, if the base of the triangle is 2 feet and the height is 4 feet, then the area is 4 square feet. The following equation shows the formula used to calculate the area of the triangle:

$$A = \frac{1}{2}bh = \frac{1}{2}(2)(4) = 4 \text{ square feet}$$

The area of a square is the length of a side squared, and the area of a rectangle is length multiplied by the width. For example, if the length of the square is 7 centimeters, then the area is 49 square centimeters. The formula for this example is $A = s^2 = 7^2 = 49$ square centimeters. An example is if the rectangle has a length of 6 inches and a width of 7 inches, then the area is 42 square inches:

$$A = lw = 6(7) = 42 \text{ square inches}$$

The area of a trapezoid is ½ the height times the sum of the bases. For example, if the length of the bases are 2.5 and 3 feet and the height 3.5 feet, then the area is 9.625 square feet. The following formula shows how the area is calculated:

$$A = \frac{1}{2}h(b_1 + b_2) = \frac{1}{2}(3.5)(2.5 + 3) = \frac{1}{2}(3.5)(5.5) = 9.625 \text{ square feet}$$

The perimeter of a figure is measured in single units, while the area is measured in square units.

A special quadrilateral is one in which both pairs of opposite sides are parallel. This type of quadrilateral is known as a *parallelogram*. A parallelogram has six important properties:

- Opposite sides are congruent.
- Opposite angles are congruent.
- Within a parallelogram, consecutive angles are supplementary, so their measurements total 180 degrees.
- If one angle is a right angle, all of them have to be right angles.
- The diagonals of the angles bisect each other.
- These diagonals form two congruent triangles.

A parallelogram with four congruent sides is a *rhombus*. A quadrilateral containing only one set of parallel sides is known as a *trapezoid*. The parallel sides are known as bases and the other two sides are known as legs. If the legs are congruent, the trapezoid can be labelled an *isosceles trapezoid*. An important property of a trapezoid is that their diagonals are congruent. Also, the median of a trapezoid is parallel to the bases, and its length is equal to half of the sum of the base lengths.

Rectangles, squares, and rhombuses are *polygons* with four sides. By definition, all rectangles are parallelograms, but only some rectangles are squares. However, some parallelograms are rectangles. Also, it's true that all squares are rectangles, and some rhombuses are squares. There are no rectangles, squares, or rhombuses that are trapezoids though, because they have more than one set of parallel sides.

Following is a *Venn diagram* that represents the relationships among quadrilaterals:

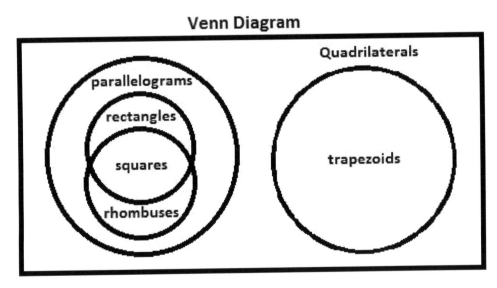

If a quadrilateral is inscribed in a circle, the sum of its opposite angles is 180 degrees. Consider the quadrilateral ABCD centered at the point O:

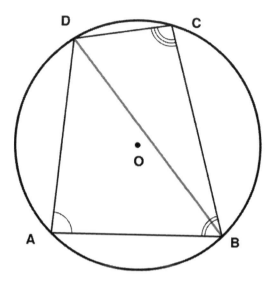

Each of the four line segments within the quadrilateral is a chord of the circle. Consider the diagonal DB. Angle DAB is an inscribed angle leaning on the arc DCB. Therefore, angle DAB is half the measure of the arc DCB. Conversely, angle DCB is an inscribed angle leaning on the arc DAB. Therefore, angle DCB is half the measure of the arc DAB. The sum of arcs DCB and DAB is 360 degrees because they make up the entire circle. Therefore, the sum of angles DAB and DCB equals half of 360 degrees, which is 180 degrees.

A *tangent line* is a line that touches a curve at a single point without going through it. A *compass* and a *straight edge* are the tools necessary to construct a tangent line from a point *P* outside the circle to the circle. A tangent line is constructed by drawing a line segment from the center of the circle *O* to the point *P*, and then finding its midpoint *M* by bisecting the line segment. By using *M* as the center, a compass is used to draw a circle through points *O* and *P*. *N* is defined as the intersection of the two circles. Finally, a line segment is drawn through *P* and *N*. This is the tangent line. Each point on a circle has only one tangent line, which is perpendicular to the radius at that point. A line similar to a tangent line is a *secant line.* Instead of intersecting the circle at one point, a secant line intersects the circle at two points. A *chord* is a smaller portion of a secant line.

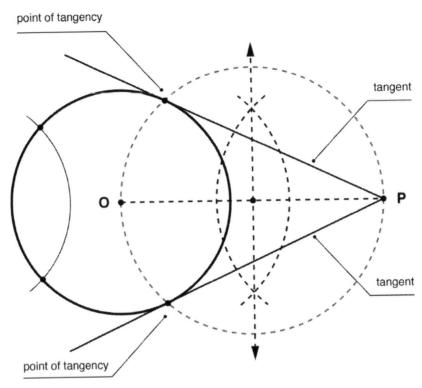

A *sector* of a circle is a portion of the circle that's enclosed by two radii and an arc. It resembles a piece of a pie, and the area of a sector can be derived using known definitions. The area of a circle can be calculated using the formula $A = \pi r^2$, where r is the radius of the circle. The area of a sector of a circle is a fraction of that calculation. For example, if the central angle θ is known in radians, the area of a sector is defined as:

$$A_s = \pi r^2 \frac{\theta}{2\pi} = \frac{\vartheta r^2}{2}$$

If the angle θ in degrees is known, the area of the sector is $A_s = \frac{\vartheta \pi r^2}{360}$. Finally, if the arc length L is known, the area of the sector can be reduced to $A_s = \frac{rL}{2}$.

Supplementary angles add up to 180 degrees. *Vertical angles* are two nonadjacent angles formed by two intersecting lines. For example, in the following picture, angles 4 and 2 are vertical angles and so are angles 1 and 3:

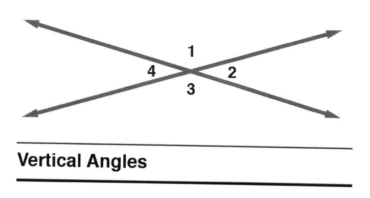

Vertical Angles

Corresponding angles are two angles in the same position whenever a straight line (known as a *transversal*) crosses two others. If the two lines are parallel, the corresponding angles are equal. In the following diagram, angles 1 and 3 are corresponding angles but aren't equal to each other:

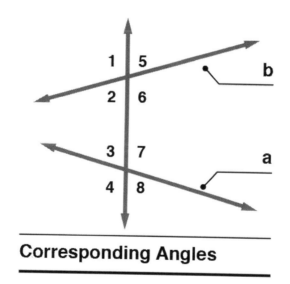

Corresponding Angles

Alternate interior angles are also a pair of angles formed when two lines are crossed by a transversal. They are opposite angles that exist inside of the two lines. In the corresponding angles diagram above, angles 2 and 7 are alternate interior angles, as well as angles 6 and 3. *Alternate exterior angles* are opposite angles formed by a transversal but, in contrast to interior angles, exterior angles exist outside the two original lines. Therefore, angles 1 and 8 are alternate exterior angles and so are angles 5 and 4. Finally, *consecutive interior angles* are pairs of angles formed by a transversal. These angles are located on the same side of the transversal and inside the two original lines. Therefore, angles 2 and 3 are a pair of consecutive interior angles, and so are angles 6 and 7. These definitions are instrumental in solving many problems that involve determining relationships between angles.

The Pythagorean Theorem

The *Pythagorean theorem* is an important relationship between the three sides of a right triangle. It states that the square of the side opposite the right triangle, known as the *hypotenuse* (denoted as c^2), is equal to the sum of the squares of the other two sides ($a^2 + b^2$). Thus, $a^2 + b^2 = c^2$.

The theorem can be seen in the following image:

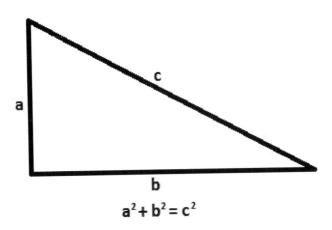

$$a^2 + b^2 = c^2$$

Both the trigonometric functions and the Pythagorean theorem can be used in problems that involve finding either a missing side or a missing angle of a right triangle. To do so, one must look to see what sides and angles are given and select the correct relationship that will help find the missing value. These relationships can also be used to solve application problems involving right triangles. Often, it's helpful to draw a figure to represent the problem to see what's missing.

Transformations in the Plane, Including Reflections, Translations, Rotations, and Dilations

Transformations in the Plane

A *transformation* occurs when a shape is altered in the plane where it exists. There are three major types of transformation: translations, reflections, and rotations. A *translation* consists of shifting a shape in one direction. A *reflection* results when a shape is transformed over a line to its mirror image. Finally, a *rotation* occurs when a shape moves in a circular motion around a specified point. The object can be turned clockwise or counterclockwise and, if rotated 360 degrees, returns to its original location.

Distance and Angle Measure

The three major types of transformations preserve distance and angle measurement. The shapes stay the same, but they are moved to another place in the plane. Therefore, the distance between any two points on the shape doesn't change. Also, any original angle measure between two line segments doesn't change. However, there are transformations that don't preserve distance and angle measurements, including those that don't preserve the original shape. For example, transformations that involve stretching and shrinking shapes don't preserve distance and angle measures. In these cases, the input variables are multiplied by either a number greater than one (*stretch*) or less than one (*shrink*).

Rigid Motion

A *rigid motion* is a transformation that preserves distance and length. Every line segment in the resulting image is congruent to the corresponding line segment in the pre-image. Congruence between two figures means a series of transformations (or a rigid motion) can be defined that maps one of the figures onto the other. Basically, two figures are congruent if they have the same shape and size.

Dilation

A shape is dilated, or a *dilation* occurs, when each side of the original image is multiplied by a given scale factor. If the scale factor is less than 1 and greater than 0, the dilation contracts the shape and the resulting shape is smaller. If the scale factor equals 1, the resulting shape is the same size and the dilation is a rigid motion. Finally, if the scale factor is greater than 1, the resulting shape is larger and the dilation expands the shape. The *center of dilation* is the point where the distance from it to any point on the new shape equals the scale factor times the distance from the center to the corresponding point in the pre-image. Dilation isn't an isometric transformation because distance isn't preserved. However, angle measure, parallel lines, and points on a line all remain unchanged. This following figure is an example of translation, rotation, dilation, and reflection:

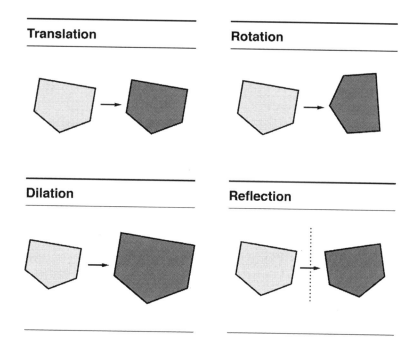

Determining Congruence

Two figures are congruent if there is a rigid motion that can map one figure onto the other. Therefore, all pairs of sides and angles within the image and pre-image must be congruent. For example, in triangles, each pair of the three sides and three angles must be congruent. Similarly, in two four-sided figures, each pair of the four sides and four angles must be congruent.

Using Equations of Circles

Degrees are used to express the size of an angle. A complete circle is represented by 360°, and a half circle is represented by 180°. In addition, a right angle fills one quarter of a circle and is represented by 90°.

Radians are another way to denote angles in terms of π, rather than degrees. A complete circle is represented by 2π radians. The formula used to convert degrees to radians is:

$$Radians = \frac{degrees \times \pi}{180}$$

For example, to convert 270 degrees to radians:

$$Radians = \frac{270 \times \pi}{180} = 4.71$$

The *arc of a circle* is the distance between two points on the circle. The length of the arc of a circle in terms of *degrees* is easily determined if the value of the central angle is known. The length of the arc is simply the value of the central angle. In this example, the length of the arc of the circle in degrees is 75°.

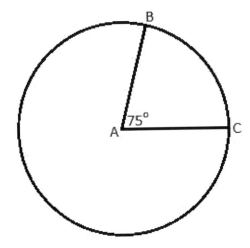

To determine the length of the arc of a circle in *distance*, the student will need to know the values for both the central angle and the radius. This formula is:

$$\frac{central\ angle}{360°} = \frac{arc\ length}{2\pi r}$$

The equation is simplified by cross-multiplying to solve for the arc length.

In the following example, the student should substitute the values of the central angle (75°) and the radius (10 inches) into the equation above to solve for the arc length.

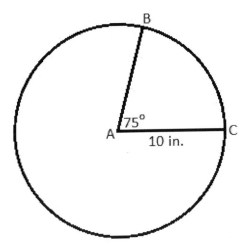

$$\frac{75°}{360°} = \frac{arc\ length}{2(3.14)(10in.)}$$

To solve the equation, first cross-multiply: 4710 = 360 (arc length). Next, divide each side of the equation by 360. The result of the formula is that the arc length is 13.1 (rounded). Please note that arc length is often referred to as *s*.

The equation used to find the area of a circle is $A = \pi r^2$. For example, if a circle has a radius of 5 centimeters, the area is computed by substituting 5 for the radius: $(5)^2$. Using this reasoning, to find half of the area of a circle, the formula is $A = .5\pi r^2$. Similarly, to find the quarter of an area of a circle, the formula is $A = .25\pi r^2$. To find any fractional area of a circle, a student can use the formula $A = \frac{C}{360}\pi r^2$, where *C* is the number of degrees of the central angle of the sector. The area of a circle can also be found by using the arc length rather than the degree of the sector. This formula is $A = rs^2$, where *s* is the arc length and *r* is the radius of the circle.

A chord is a line that connects two points on a circle's circumference. If the radius and the value of the angle subtended at the center by the chord is known, the formula to find the chord length is: $C = 2 \times radius \times \sin\frac{angle}{2}$. Remember that this formula is based on half the length of the chord, so the radius is doubled to determine the full length of the chord.

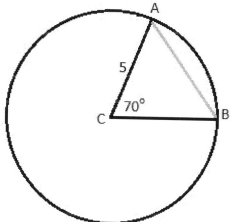

For example, the radius in the diagram above is 5 and the angle is 70 degrees. To find the chord length, plug in the values for the radius and angle to obtain the answer of 5.7.

$$5 \times \sin\frac{70}{2} = 5.7$$

Chords that intersect each other at a point within a circle are related. The intersecting chord theorem states that when two chords intersect, each is cut into two portions or segments. The products of the two segments of each respective chord are equal to one another.

Other related concepts for circles include the diameter and circumference. *Circumference* is the distance around a circle. The formula for circumference is $C = 2\pi r$. The *diameter* of a circle is the distance across a circle through its center point. The formula for circumference can also be thought of as $C = dr$ where *d* is the circle's diameter, since the diameter of a circle is *2r*.

A *circle* can be defined as the set of all points that are the same distance (known as the radius, *r*) from a single point *C* (known as the center of the circle). The center has coordinates (h, k), and any point on the circle can be labelled with coordinates (x, y).

135

As shown below, a *right triangle* is formed with these two points:

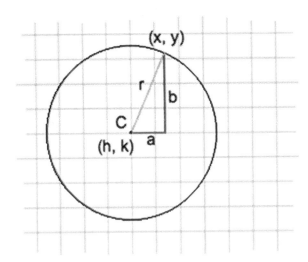

The Pythagorean theorem states that $a^2 + b^2 = r^2$. However, a can be replaced by $|x - h|$ and b can be replaced by $|y - k|$ by using the *distance formula* which is:

$$d = \sqrt{(x_2 - x_1)^2 + (y_2 - y_1)^2}$$

That substitution results in:

$$(x - h)^2 + (y - k)^2 = r^2$$

This is the formula for finding the equation of any circle with a center (h, k) and a radius r. Note that sometimes C is used instead of r.

The *radius* of a circle is the distance from the center of the circle to any point on the circle. A *chord* of a circle is a straight line formed when its endpoints are allowed to be on any two points on the circle. Many angles exist within a circle. A *central angle* is formed by using two radii as its rays and the center of the circle as its vertex. An *inscribed angle* is formed by using two chords as its rays, and its vertex is a point on the circle itself. Finally, a *circumscribed angle* has a vertex that is a point outside the circle and rays that intersect with the circle. Some relationships exist between these types of angles, and, in order to define these relationships, arc measure must be understood. An *arc* of a circle is a portion of the circumference. Finding the *arc measure* is the same as finding the degree measure of the central angle that intersects the circle to form the arc. The measure of an inscribed angle is half the measure of its intercepted arc. It's also true that the measure of a circumscribed angle is equal to 180 degrees minus the measure of the central angle that forms the arc in the angle.

Properties of Lines, Including Parallel, Perpendicular, and Midpoint of Line Segments

In geometry, a *line* connects two points, has no thickness, and extends indefinitely in both directions beyond each point. If the length is finite, it's known as a *line segment* and has two *endpoints*. A *ray* is the straight portion of a line that has one endpoint and extends indefinitely in the other direction. An *angle* is formed when two rays begin at the same endpoint and extend indefinitely. The endpoint of an angle is called a *vertex*. *Adjacent angles* are two side-by-side angles formed from the same ray that have the same endpoint. Angles are measured in *degrees* or *radians*, which is a measure of *rotation*. A *full rotation* equals 360 degrees or 2π radians, which represents a circle. Half a rotation equals 180 degrees or π radians and represents a half-circle. Subsequently, 90 degrees ($\frac{\pi}{2}$ radians) represents a quarter of a circle, which is known as a *right angle*. Any angle less than 90 degrees is an *acute angle*, and any angle greater than 90 degrees is an *obtuse angle*. Angle measurement is additive. When an angle is broken into two non-overlapping angles, the total measure of the larger angle equals the sum of the two smaller angles. Lines are *coplanar* if they're located in the same plane. Two lines are *parallel* if they are coplanar, extend in the same direction, and never cross. If lines do cross, they're labeled as *intersecting lines* because they "intersect" at one point. If they intersect at more than one point, they're the same line. *Perpendicular lines* are coplanar lines that form a right angle at their point of intersection.

Rotations, reflections, and translations are *isometric transformations*, because throughout each transformation the distance of line segments is maintained, the angle measure is maintained, parallel lines in the original shape remain parallel, and points on lines remain on those lines. A rotation turns a shape around a specific point (*O*) known as the *center of rotation*. An *angle of rotation* is formed by drawing a ray from the center of rotation to a point (*P*) on the original shape and to the point's image (*P'*) on the reflected shape. Thus, it's true that *OP=OP'*. A reflection over a line (*l*), known as the *line of reflection*, takes an original point P and maps it to its image P' on the opposite side of *l*. The line of reflection is the perpendicular bisector of every line formed by an original point and its image. A translation maps each point P in the original shape to a new point P'. The line segment formed between each point and its image consists of the same length, and the line segment formed by two original points is parallel to the line segment formed from their two images.

As mentioned, two lines are parallel if they have the same slope. Two lines are perpendicular if the product of their slope equals -1. Parallel lines never intersect unless they are the same line, and perpendicular lines intersect at a right angle. If two lines aren't parallel, they must intersect at one point. Determining equations of lines based on properties of parallel and perpendicular lines appears in word problems. To find an equation of a line, both the slope and a point the line goes through are necessary. Therefore, if an equation of a line is needed that's parallel to a given line and runs through a specified point, the slope of the given line and the point are plugged into the point-slope form of an equation of a line. Secondly, if an equation of a line is needed that's perpendicular to a given line running through a specified point, the negative reciprocal of the slope of the given line and the point are plugged into the point-slope form. Also, if the point of intersection of two lines is known, that point will be used to solve the set of equations. Therefore, to solve a system of equations, the point of intersection must be found. If a set of two equations with two unknown variables has no solution, the lines are parallel.

Sine, Cosine, and Tangent to Solve Simple Problems Involving Right Triangle Trigonometry

Within similar triangles, corresponding sides are proportional and angles are congruent. In addition, within similar triangles, the ratio of the side lengths is the same. This property is true even if side lengths are different. Within right triangles, trigonometric ratios can be defined for the acute angle within the triangle. The functions can be seen here:

Table for trigonometric functions

$\sin 0 = 0$	$\cos 0 = 1$	$\tan 0 = 0$
$\sin \dfrac{\pi}{6} = \dfrac{1}{2}$	$\cos \dfrac{\pi}{6} = \dfrac{\sqrt{3}}{2}$	$\tan \dfrac{\pi}{6} = \dfrac{\sqrt{3}}{3}$
$\sin \dfrac{\pi}{4} = \dfrac{\sqrt{2}}{2}$	$\cos \dfrac{\pi}{4} = \dfrac{\sqrt{2}}{2}$	$\tan \dfrac{\pi}{4} = 1$
$\sin \dfrac{\pi}{3} = \dfrac{\sqrt{3}}{2}$	$\cos \dfrac{\pi}{3} = \dfrac{1}{2}$	$\tan \dfrac{\pi}{3} = \sqrt{3}$
$\sin \dfrac{\pi}{2} = 1$	$\cos \dfrac{\pi}{2} = 0$	$\tan \dfrac{\pi}{2} = undefined$
$\csc 0 = undefined$	$\sec 0 = 1$	$\cot 0 = undefined$
$\csc \dfrac{\pi}{6} = 2$	$\sec \dfrac{\pi}{6} = \dfrac{2\sqrt{3}}{3}$	$\cot \dfrac{\pi}{6} = \sqrt{3}$
$\csc \dfrac{\pi}{4} = \sqrt{2}$	$\sec \dfrac{\pi}{4} = \sqrt{2}$	$\cot \dfrac{\pi}{4} = 1$
$\csc \dfrac{\pi}{3} = \dfrac{2\sqrt{3}}{3}$	$\sec \dfrac{\pi}{3} = 2$	$\cot \dfrac{\pi}{3} = \dfrac{\sqrt{3}}{3}$
$\csc \dfrac{\pi}{2} = 1$	$\sec \dfrac{\pi}{2} = undefined$	$\cot \dfrac{\pi}{2} = 0$

Note that expanding or shrinking the triangle won't change the ratios. However, changing the angle measurements will alter the calculations. Mnemonic devices exist to help remember these trigonometric functions, and a popular choice is *SOHCAHTOA* which is short for *Sine = Opposite/Hypotenuse, Cosine = Adjacent/Hypotenuse, and Tangent = Opposite/Adjacent*

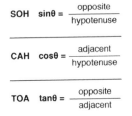
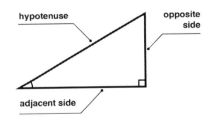

Angles that add up to 90 degrees are *complementary*. Within a right triangle, two complementary angles exist because the third angle is always 90 degrees. In this scenario, the *sine* of one of the complementary angles is equal to the *cosine* of the other angle. The opposite is also true. This relationship exists because sine and cosine will be calculated as the ratios of the same side lengths.

A triangle that isn't a right triangle is known as an *oblique triangle*. It should be noted that even if the triangle consists of three acute angles, it is still referred to as an obtuse triangle. *Obtuse*, in this case, does not refer to an angle measurement. Consider the following oblique triangle:

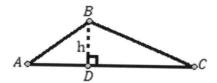

For this triangle, $Area = \frac{1}{2} \times base \times height = \frac{1}{2} \times AC \times BD$. The auxiliary line drawn from the vertex B perpendicular to the opposite side AC represents the height of the triangle. This line splits the larger triangle into two smaller right triangles, which allows for the use of the trigonometric functions (specifically that $\sin A = \frac{h}{AB}$). Therefore, $Area = \frac{1}{2} \times AC \times AB \times \sin A$. Typically the sides are labelled as the lowercase letter of the vertex that's opposite. Therefore, the formula can be written as $Area = \frac{1}{2} ab \sin A$. This area formula can be used to find areas of triangles when given side lengths and angle measurements, or it can be used to find side lengths or angle measurements based on a specific area and other characteristics of the triangle.

The *law of sines* and *law of cosines* are two more relationships that exist within oblique triangles. Consider a triangle with sides *a*, *b*, and *c*, and angles *A*, *B*, and *C* opposite the corresponding sides:

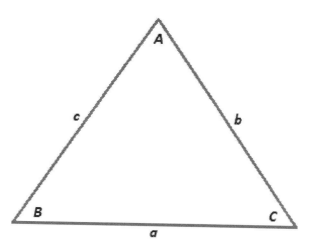

The law of cosine states that $c^2 = a^2 + b^2 - 2ab \cos C$. The law of sines states that $\frac{\sin A}{a} = \frac{\sin B}{b} = \frac{\sin C}{c}$. In addition to the area formula, these two relationships can help find unknown angle and side measurements in oblique triangles.

Trigonometric functions are periodic. Both sine and cosine have period 2π. For each input angle value, the output value follows around the unit circle. Once it reaches the starting point, it continues around and around the circle. It is true that:

$$\sin(0) = \sin(2\pi) = \sin(4\pi), \text{ etc.}$$

and

$$\cos(0) = \cos(2\pi) = \cos(4\pi)$$

Tangent has period π, and its output values repeat themselves every half of the unit circle. The domain of sine and cosine are all real numbers, and the domain of tangent is all real numbers, except the points where cosine equals zero. It is also true that:

$$\sin(-x) = -\sin x$$

$$\cos(-x) = \cos(x)$$

$$\tan(-x) = -\tan(x)$$

So sine and tangent are odd functions, while cosine is an even function. Sine and tangent are symmetric with respect to the origin, and cosine is symmetric with respect to the y-axis.

The graph of trigonometric functions can be used to model different situations. General forms are

$$y = a \sin b(x - h) + k$$

and

$$y = a \cos b (x - h) + k$$

The variable a represents the amplitude, which shows the maximum and minimum value of the function. The b is used to find the period by using the ratio $\frac{2\pi}{b}$, h is the horizontal shift, and k is the vertical shift.

The equation $y = \sin(x)$ is shown on the following graph with the thick black line. The stretched graph of $y = 2\sin(x)$ is shown in solid black, and the shrunken graph $y = \frac{1}{2}\sin(x)$ is shown with the dotted line.

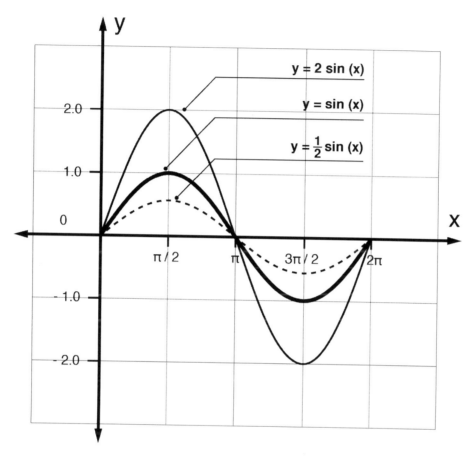

Trigonometric functions are used to find unknown ratios for a given angle measure. The inverse of these trig functions is used to find the unknown angle, given a ratio. For example, the expression $\arcsin(\frac{1}{2})$ means finding the value of x for $\sin(x) = \frac{1}{2}$. Since $\sin(\theta) = \frac{y}{1}$ on the unit circle, the angle whose y-value is $\frac{1}{2}$ is $\frac{\pi}{6}$. The inverse of any of the trigonometric functions can be used to find a missing angle measurement. Values not found on the unit circle can be found using the trigonometric functions on the calculator, making sure its mode is set to degrees or radians.

In order for the inverse to exist, the function must be one-to-one over its domain. There cannot be two input values connected to the same output. For example, the following graphs show the functions $y =$

cos(x) and $y = \arccos(x)$. In order to have an inverse, the domain of cosine is restricted from 0 to π. Therefore, the range of its inverse function is $[0, \pi]$.

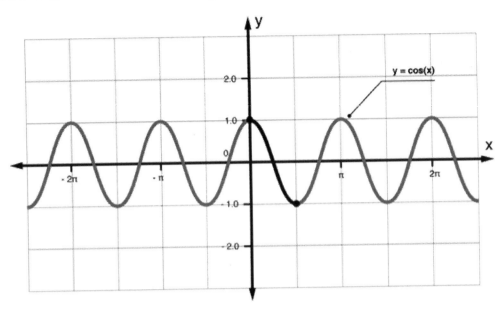

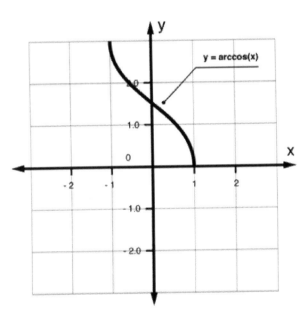

Inverses of trigonometric functions can be used to solve real-world problems. For example, there are many situations where the lengths of a perceived triangle can be found, but the angles are unknown. Consider a problem where the height of a flag (25 feet) and the distance on the ground to the flag is given (42 feet). The unknown, x, is the angle. To find this angle, the equation $\tan x = \frac{42}{25}$ is used. To solve for x, the inverse function can be used to turn the equation into $\tan^{-1} \frac{42}{25} = x$. Using the calculator, in degree mode, the answer is found to be $x = 59.2$ degrees.

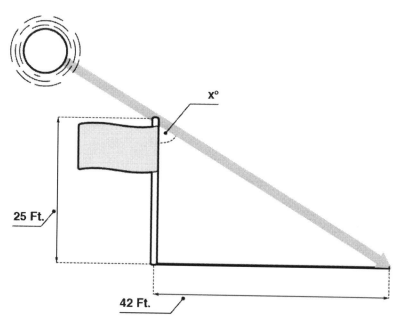

Trigonometric Identities

From the unit circle, the trigonometric ratios were found for the special right triangle with a hypotenuse of 1.

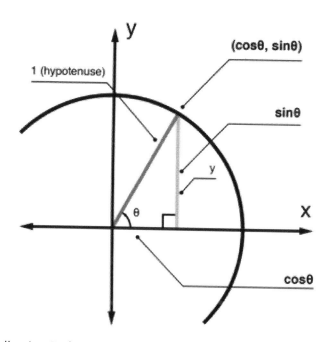

From this triangle, the following Pythagorean identities are formed:

$$\sin^2 \theta + \cos^2 \theta = 1$$

$$\tan^2 \theta + 1 = \sec^2 \theta$$

$$1 + \cot^2 \theta = \csc^2 \theta$$

The second two identities are formed by manipulating the first identity. Since identities are statements that are true for any value of the variable, then they may be used to manipulate equations. For example, a problem may ask for simplification of the expression $\cos^2 x + \cos^2 x \tan^2 x$. Using the fact that

$$\tan(x) = \frac{\sin x}{\cos x}$$

$\frac{\sin^2 x}{\cos^2 x}$ can then be substituted in for $\tan^2 x$, making the expression:

$$\cos^2 x + \cos^2 x \frac{\sin^2 x}{\cos^2 x}$$

Then the two $\cos^2 x$ terms on top and bottom cancel each other out, simplifying the expression to:

$$\cos^2 x + \sin^2 x$$

By the first Pythagorean identity stated above, the expression can be turned into:

$$\cos^2 x + \sin^2 x = 1$$

Another set of trigonometric identities are the double-angle formulas:

$$\sin 2\alpha = 2 \sin \alpha \cos \alpha$$

$$\cos 2\alpha = \begin{cases} \cos^2\alpha - \sin^2\alpha \\ 2\cos^2\alpha - 1 \\ 1 - 2\sin^2\alpha \end{cases}$$

Using these formulas, the following identity can be proved:

$$\sin 2x = \frac{2 \tan x}{1 + \tan^2 x}$$

By using one of the Pythagorean identities, the denominator can be rewritten as:

$$1 + \tan^2 x = \sec^2 x$$

By knowing the reciprocals of the trigonometric identities, the secant term can be rewritten to form the equation:

$$\sin 2x = \frac{2 \tan x}{1} \times \cos^2 x$$

Replacing $\tan(x)$, the equation becomes:

$$\sin 2x = \frac{2 \sin x}{\cos x} \times \cos^2 x$$

The $\cos x$ can cancel out. The new equation is:

$$\sin 2x = 2 \sin x \times \cos x$$

This final equation is one of the double-angle formulas.

Other trigonometric identities such as half-angle formulas, sum and difference formulas, and difference of angles formulas can be used to prove and rewrite trigonometric equations. Depending on the given equation or expression, the correct identities need to be chosen to write equivalent statements.

The graph of sine is equal to the graph of cosine, shifted $\frac{\pi}{2}$ units. Therefore, the function $y = \sin x$ is equal to:

$$y = \cos(\frac{\pi}{2} - x)$$

Within functions, adding a constant to the independent variable shifts the graph either left or right. By shifting the cosine graph, the curve lies on top of the sine function. By transforming the function, the two equations give the same output for any given input.

Functions of Two Variables

The graph of a function of one variable can be represented in the xy-plane and is known as a *curve*. When a function has two variables, the function is graphed in three-dimensional space, and the graph is known as a *surface*. The graph is the set of all ordered triples (x, y, z) that satisfy the function. Within three-dimensional space, there is a third axis known as the z-axis.

Solving Trigonometric Functions

Solving trigonometric functions can be done with a knowledge of the unit circle and the trigonometric identities. It requires the use of opposite operations combined with trigonometric ratios for special triangles. For example, the problem may require solving the equation $2 \cos^2 x - \sqrt{3} \cos x = 0$ for the values of x between zero and 180 degrees. The first step is to factor out the $\cos x$ term, resulting in:

$$\cos x (2 \cos x - \sqrt{3}) = 0$$

By the factoring method of solving, each factor can be set equal to zero:

$$\cos x = 0$$

$$(2 \cos x - \sqrt{3}) = 0$$

The second equation can be solved to yield the following equation:

$$\cos x = \frac{\sqrt{3}}{2}$$

Now that the value of x is found, the trigonometric ratios can be used to find the solutions of $x = 0$ and 90 degrees.

Solving trigonometric functions requires the use of algebra to isolate the variable and a knowledge of trigonometric ratios to find the value of the variable. The unit circle can be used to find answers for special triangles. Beyond those triangles, a calculator can be used to solve for variables within the trigonometric functions.

Perimeter, Area, Surface Area, and Volume Formulas

Circumference and Volume

The *circumference* of a circle is found by calculating the perimeter of the shape. The ratio of the circumference to the diameter of the circle is π, so the formula for circumference is $C = \pi d = 2\pi r$. To visualize this, one can imagine that a circle is a pie divided into an equal number of slices. The slices can be aligned to form a parallelogram with a height equal to the radius r, and a base equal to half of the circumference of the circle πr. Plugging these expressions into the formula for area of a parallelogram results in $A = bh = \pi r^2$. The *volume* of a cylinder is then found by adding a third dimension onto the circle. Volume of a cylinder is calculated by multiplying the area of the base (which is a circle) by the height of the cylinder. Doing so results in the equation $V = \pi r^2 h$. Next, consider the volume of a rectangular box $= lwh$, where l is length, w is width, and h is height. This can be simplified into $V = Ah$, where A is the area of the base. The *volume* of a pyramid with the same dimensions is $\frac{1}{3}$ of this quantity because it fills up $\frac{1}{3}$ of the space. Therefore, the volume of a pyramid is $V = \frac{1}{3}Ah$. In a similar fashion, the volume of a cone is $\frac{1}{3}$ of the volume of a cylinder. Therefore, the formula for the volume of a cone is $\frac{1}{3}\pi r^2 h$.

Perimeter and Area

Both the perimeter and area formulas are applicable in real-world scenarios. Knowing the *perimeter* is useful when the length of a shape's outline is needed. For example, to build a fence around a yard, the yard's perimeter must be calculated so enough materials are purchased to complete the fence. The *area* is necessary anytime the surface of a shape is needed. For example, when constructing a garden, the area of the garden region is needed so enough dirt can be purchased to fill it. Many times, it's necessary to break up the given shape into shapes with known perimeter and area formulas (such as triangles and rectangles) and add the individual perimeters or areas together to determine the desired quantity.

Concepts of Density Based on Area and Volume in Modeling Situations

The *density* of a substance is the ratio of mass to area or volume. It's a relationship between the mass and how much space the object actually takes up. Knowing which units to use in each situation is crucial. Population density is an example of a real-life situation that's modeled by using density concepts. It involves calculating the ratio of the number of people to the number of square miles. The amount of material needed per a specific unit of area or volume is another application. For example, estimating the number of BTUs per cubic foot of a home is a measurement that relates to heating or cooling the house based on the desired temperature and the house's size.

Practice Questions

1. If a car can travel 300 miles in 4 hours, how far can it go in an hour and a half?
   a. 100 miles
   b. 112.5 miles
   c. 135.5 miles
   d. 150 miles

2. At the store, Jan spends $90 on apples and oranges. Apples cost $1 each and oranges cost $2 each. If Jan buys the same number of apples as oranges, how many oranges did she buy?
   a. 20
   b. 25
   c. 30
   d. 35

3. What is the volume of a box with rectangular sides 5 feet long, 6 feet wide, and 3 feet high?
   a. 60 cubic feet
   b. 75 cubic feet
   c. 90 cubic feet
   d. 14 cubic feet

4. A train traveling 50 miles per hour takes a trip lasting 3 hours. If a map has a scale of 1 inch per 10 miles, how many inches apart are the train's starting point and ending point on the map?
   a. 14
   b. 12
   c. 13
   d. 15

5. A traveler takes an hour to drive to a museum, spends 3 hours and 30 minutes there, and takes half an hour to drive home. What percentage of his or her time was spent driving?
   a. 15%
   b. 30%
   c. 40%
   d. 60%

6. A truck is carrying three cylindrical barrels. Their bases have a diameter of 2 feet and they have a height of 3 feet. What is the total volume of the three barrels in cubic feet?
   a. 3π
   b. 9π
   c. 12π
   d. 15π

7. Greg buys a $10 lunch with 5% sales tax. He leaves a $2 tip after his bill. How much money does he spend?
   a. $12.50
   b. $12
   c. $13
   d. $13.25

8. Marty wishes to save $150 over a 4-day period. How much must Marty save each day on average?
   a. $37.50
   b. $35
   c. $45.50
   d. $41

9. Bernard can make $80 per day. If he needs to make $300 and only works full days, how many days will this take?
   a. 6
   b. 3
   c. 5
   d. 4

10. A couple buys a house for $150,000. They sell it for $165,000. By what percentage did the house's value increase?
   a. 10%
   b. 13%
   c. 15%
   d. 17%

11. A school has 15 teachers and 20 teaching assistants. They have 200 students. What is the ratio of faculty to students?
   a. 3:20
   b. 4:17
   c. 5:54
   d. 7:40

12. A map has a scale of 1 inch per 5 miles. A car can travel 60 miles per hour. If the distance from the start to the destination is 3 inches on the map, how long will it take the car to make the trip?
   a. 12 minutes
   b. 15 minutes
   c. 17 minutes
   d. 20 minutes

13. Taylor works two jobs. The first pays $20,000 per year. The second pays $10,000 per year. She donates 15% of her income to charity. How much does she donate each year?
   a. $4500
   b. $5000
   c. $5500
   d. $6000

14. A box with rectangular sides is 24 inches wide, 18 inches deep, and 12 inches high. What is the volume of the box in cubic feet?
   a. 2
   b. 3
   c. 4
   d. 5

15. Kristen purchases $100 worth of CDs and DVDs. The CDs cost $10 each and the DVDs cost $15. If she bought four DVDs, how many CDs did she buy?

    a. 5
    b. 6
    c. 3
    d. 4

16. If Sarah reads at an average rate of 21 pages in four nights, how long will it take her to read 140 pages?

    a. 6 nights
    b. 26 nights
    c. 8 nights
    d. 27 nights

17. Mom's car drove 72 miles in 90 minutes. There are 5280 feet per mile. How fast did she drive in feet per second?

    a. 0.8 feet per second
    b. 48.9 feet per second
    c. 0.009 feet per second
    d. 70. 4 feet per second

18. This chart indicates how many sales of CDs, vinyl records, and MP3 downloads occurred over the last year. Approximately what percentage of the total sales was from CDs?

    a. 55%
    b. 25%
    c. 40%
    d. 5%

19. After a 20% sale discount, Frank purchased a new refrigerator for $850. How much did he save from the original price?

    a. $170
    b. $212.50
    c. $105.75
    d. $200

20. 3.4+2.35+4=
    a. 5.35
    b. 9.2
    c. 9.75
    d. 10.25

21. $5.88 \times 3.2 =$
    a. 18.816
    b. 16.44
    c. 20.352
    d. 17

22. $\frac{3}{25} =$
    a. 0.15
    b. 0.1
    c. 0.9
    d. 0.12

23. Which of the following is largest?
    a. 0.45
    b. 0.096
    c. 0.3
    d. 0.313

24. Which of the following is NOT a way to write 40 percent of N?
    a. $(0.4)N$
    b. $\frac{2}{5}N$
    c. $40N$
    d. $\frac{4N}{10}$

25. Which is closest to 17.8×9.9?
    a. 140
    b. 180
    c. 200
    d. 350

26. A student gets an 85% on a test with 20 questions. How many answers did the student solve correctly?
    a. 15
    b. 16
    c. 17
    d. 18

27. Four people split a bill. The first person pays for $\frac{1}{5}$, the second person pays for $\frac{1}{4}$, and the third person pays for $\frac{1}{3}$. What fraction of the bill does the fourth person pay?

    a. $\frac{13}{60}$

    b. $\frac{47}{60}$

    c. $\frac{1}{4}$

    d. $\frac{4}{15}$

28. 6 is 30% of what number?

    a. 18

    b. 20

    c. 24

    d. 26

29. $3\frac{2}{3} - 1\frac{4}{5} =$

    a. $1\frac{13}{15}$

    b. $\frac{14}{15}$

    c. $2\frac{2}{3}$

    d. $\frac{4}{5}$

30. What is $\frac{420}{98}$ rounded to the nearest integer?

    a. 4

    b. 3

    c. 5

    d. 6

31. $4\frac{1}{3} + 3\frac{3}{4} =$

    a. $6\frac{5}{12}$

    b. $8\frac{1}{12}$

    c. $8\frac{2}{3}$

    d. $7\frac{7}{12}$

32. Five of six numbers have a sum of 25. The average of all six numbers is 6. What is the sixth number?

    a. 8

    b. 10

    c. 11

    d. 12

33. $52.3 \times 10^{-3} =$

    a. 0.00523

    b. 0.0523

    c. 0.523

    d. 523

34. If $\frac{5}{2} \div \frac{1}{3} = n$, then n is between:

   a. 5 and 7
   b. 7 and 9
   c. 9 and 11
   d. 3 and 5

35. A closet is filled with red, blue, and green shirts. If $\frac{1}{3}$ of the shirts are green and $\frac{2}{5}$ are red, what fraction of the shirts are blue?

   a. $\frac{4}{15}$
   b. $\frac{1}{5}$
   c. $\frac{7}{15}$
   d. $\frac{1}{2}$

36. Shawna buys $2\frac{1}{2}$ gallons of paint. If she uses $\frac{1}{3}$ of it on the first day, how much does she have left?

   a. $1\frac{5}{6}$ gallons

   b. $1\frac{1}{2}$ gallons

   c. $1\frac{2}{3}$ gallons

   d. 2 gallons

37. A drug needs to be stored at room temperature (68 °F). What is the equivalent temperature in degrees Celsius?

   a. 36 °C
   b. 72 °C
   c. 68 °C
   d. 20 °C

38. What is the slope of this line?

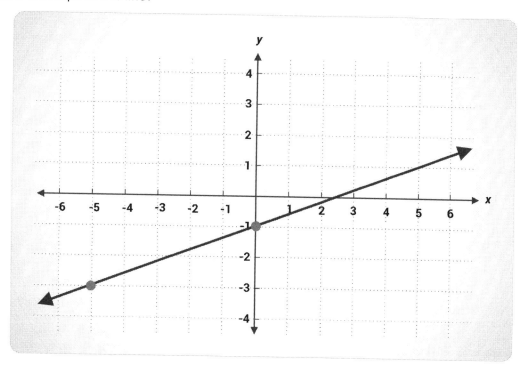

    a. 2

    b. $\frac{5}{2}$

    c. $\frac{1}{2}$

    d. $\frac{2}{5}$

39. What is the perimeter of the figure below? Note that the solid outer line is the perimeter.

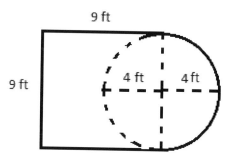

    a. 48.565 ft
    b. 39.565 ft
    c. 19.78 ft
    d. 30.565 ft

40. Which of the following equations best represents the problem below?
The width of a rectangle is 2 centimeters less than the length. If the perimeter of the rectangle is 44 centimeters, then what are the dimensions of the rectangle?

    a. $2l + 2(l - 2) = 44$
    b. $l + 2) + (l + 2) + l = 48$
    c. $l \times (l - 2) = 44$
    d. $(l + 2) + (l + 2) + l = 44$

41. How will the following algebraic expression be simplified: $(5x^2 - 3x + 4) - (2x^2 - 7)$?

    a. x^5
    b. $3x^2 - 3x + 11$
    c. $3x^2 - 3x - 3$
    d. $x - 3$

42. In Jim's school, there are 3 girls for every 2 boys. There are 650 students in total. Using this information, how many students are girls?

    a. 260
    b. 130
    c. 65
    d. 390

43. Kimberley earns $10 an hour babysitting, and after 10 p.m., she earns $12 an hour, with the amount paid being rounded to the nearest hour accordingly. On her last job, she worked from 5:30 p.m. to 11 p.m. In total, how much did Kimberley earn for that job?

    a. $45
    b. $57
    c. $62
    d. $42

44. Keith's bakery had 252 customers go through its doors last week. This week, that number increased to 378. By what percentage did his customer volume increase?

    a. 26%
    b. 50%
    c. 35%
    d. 12%

45. A family purchases a vehicle in 2005 for $20,000. In 2010, they decide to sell it for a newer model. They are able to sell the car for $8,000. By what percentage did the value of the family's car drop?

    a. 40%
    b. 68%
    c. 60%
    d. 33%

46. In May of 2010, a couple purchased a house for $100,000. In September of 2016, the couple sold the house for $93,000 so they could purchase a bigger one to start a family. How many months did they own the house?

    a. 76

    b. 54

    c. 85

    d. 93

47. At the beginning of the day, Xavier has 20 apples. At lunch, he meets his sister Emma and gives her half of his apples. After lunch, he stops by his neighbor Jim's house and gives him 6 of his apples. He then uses ¾ of his remaining apples to make an apple pie for dessert at dinner. At the end of the day, how many apples does Xavier have left?

    a. 4

    b. 6

    c. 2

    d. 1

48. What is the equation of a circle whose center is (0, 0) and whole radius is 5?

    a. $(x-5)^2 + (y-5)^2 = 25$

    b. $(x)^2 + (y)^2 = 5$

    c. $(x)^2 + (y)^2 = 25$

    d. $(x+5)^2 + (y+5)^2 = 25$

49. What is the equation of a circle whose center is (1, 5) and whole radius is 4?

    a. $(x-1)^2 + (y-25)^2 = 4$

    b. $(x-1)^2 + (y-25)^2 = 16$

    c. $(x+1)^2 + (y+5)^2 = 16$

    d. $(x-1)^2 + (y-5)^2 = 16$

50. Where does the point (-3, -4) lie on the circle with the equation $(x)^2 + (y)^2 = 25$?

    a. Inside of the circle.

    b. Outside of the circle.

    c. On the circle.

    d. There is not enough information to tell.

51. What is the volume of a cylinder, in terms of π, with a radius of 6 centimeters and a height of 2 centimeters?

    a. $36\,\pi$ cm³

    b. $24\,\pi$ cm³

    c. $72\,\pi$ cm³

    d. $48\,\pi$ cm³

52. What is the length of the hypotenuse of a right triangle with one leg equal to 3 centimeters and the other leg equal to 4 centimeters?

    a. 7 cm

    b. 5 cm

    c. 25 cm

    d. 12 cm

53. If Danny takes 48 minutes to walk 3 miles, how many minutes should it take him to walk 5 miles maintaining the same speed?

54. The perimeter of a 6-sided polygon is 56 cm. The length of three sides is 9 cm each. The length of two other sides is 8 cm each. What is the length of the missing side?

55. Convert $\frac{3}{25}$ to a decimal.

56. What is the value of $x^2 - 2xy + 2y^2$ when $x = 2, y = 3$?

57. If $4x - 3 = 5$, then $x =$

	-	-	-	-	-
		.	.	.	.
		0	0	0	0
		1	1	1	1
		2	2	2	2
		3	3	3	3
		4	4	4	4
		5	5	5	5
		6	6	6	6
		7	7	7	7
		8	8	8	8
		9	9	9	9

Answer Explanations

1. B: 300 miles in 4 hours is 300/4 = 75 miles per hour. In 1.5 hours, the car will go 1.5 × 75 miles, or 112.5 miles.

2. C: One apple/orange pair costs $3 total. Therefore, Jan bought 90/3 = 30 total pairs, and hence, she bought 30 oranges.

3. C: The formula for the volume of a box with rectangular sides is the length times width times height, so 5 × 6 × 3 = 90 cubic feet.

4. D: First, the train's journey in the real word is 3 x 50 = 150 miles. On the map, 1 inch corresponds to 10 miles, so there is 150/10 = 15 inches on the map.

5. B: The total trip time is 1 + 3.5 + 0.5 = 5 hours. The total time driving is 1 + 0.5 = 1.5 hours. So, the fraction of time spent driving is 1.5/5 or 3/10. To get the percentage, convert this to a fraction out of 100. The numerator and denominator are multiplied by 10, with a result of 30/100. The percentage is the numerator in a fraction out of 100, so 30%.

6. B: The formula for the volume of a cylinder is $\pi r^2 h$, where r is the radius and h is the height. The diameter is twice the radius, so these barrels have a radius of 1 foot. That means each barrel has a volume of $\pi \times 1^2 \times 3 = 3\pi$ cubic feet. Since there are three of them, the total is $3 \times 3\pi = 9\pi$ cubic feet.

7. A: The tip is not taxed, so he pays 5% tax only on the $10. 5% of $10 is 0.05 × 10 = $0.50. Add up $10 + $2 + $0.50 to get $12.50.

8. A: The first step is to divide up $150 into four equal parts. 150/4 is 37.5, so she needs to save an average of $37.50 per day.

9. D: 300/80 =30/8 = 15/4 =3.75. But Bernard is only working full days, so he will need to work 4 days, since 3 days is not sufficient.

10. A: The value went up by $165,000 − $150,000 = $15,000. Out of $150,000, this is $\frac{15,000}{150,000} = \frac{1}{10}$. Convert this to having a denominator of 100, the result is $\frac{10}{100}$ or 10%.

11. D: The total faculty is 15 + 20 = 35. Therefore, the faculty to student ratio is 35:200. Then, to simplify this ratio, both the numerator and the denominator are divided by 5, since 5 is a common factor of both, which yields 7:40.

12. B: The journey will be 5 × 3 = 15 miles. A car travelling at 60 miles per hour is travelling at 1 mile per minute. So, it will take 15/1 = 15 minutes to take the journey.

13. A: Taylor's total income is $20,000 + $10,000 = $30,000. 15% of this is $\frac{15}{100} = \frac{3}{20}$. So $\frac{3}{20} \times \$30,000 = \frac{90,000}{20} = \frac{9000}{2} = \$4500$.

14. B: Since the answer will be in cubic feet rather than inches, the first step is to convert from inches to feet for the dimensions of the box. There are 12 inches per foot, so the box is 24/12 = 2 feet wide, 18/12 = 1.5 feet deep, and 12/12 = 1 foot high. The volume is the product of these three together: $2 \times 1.5 \times 1 = 3$ cubic feet.

15. D: Kristen bought four DVDs, which would cost a total of $4 \times 15 = \$60$. She spent a total of $100, so she spent $100 – $60 = $40 on CDs. Since they cost $10 each, she must have purchased 40/10 = four CDs.

16. D: This problem can be solved by setting up a proportion involving the given information and the unknown value. The proportion is $\frac{21\ pages}{4\ nights} = \frac{140\ pages}{x\ nights}$. Solving the proportion by cross-multiplying, the equation becomes $21x = 4 * 140$, where $x = 26.67$. Since it is not an exact number of nights, the answer is rounded up to 27 nights. Twenty-six nights would not give Sarah enough time.

17. D: This problem can be solved by using unit conversion. The initial units are miles per minute. The final units need to be feet per second. Converting miles to feet uses the equivalence statement 1 mile = 5,280 feet. Converting minutes to seconds uses the equivalence statement 1 minute = 60 seconds. Setting up the ratios to convert the units is shown in the following equation $\frac{72\ miles}{90\ minutes} * \frac{1\ minute}{60\ seconds} * \frac{5280\ feet}{1\ mile} = 70.4$ feet per second. The initial units cancel out, and the new units are left.

18. C: The sum total percentage of a pie chart must equal 100%. Since the CD sales take up less than half of the chart and more than a quarter (25%), it can be determined to be 40% overall. This can also be measured with a protractor. The angle of a circle is 360°. Since 25% of 360 would be 90° and 50% would be 180°, the angle percentage of CD sales falls in between; therefore, it would be Choice C.

19. B: Since $850 is the price *after* a 20% discount, $850 represents 80% of the original price. To determine the original price, set up a proportion with the ratio of the sale price (850) to original price (unknown) equal to the ratio of sale percentage:

$$\frac{850}{x} = \frac{80}{100}$$

(where *x* represents the unknown original price)

To solve a proportion, cross multiply the numerators and denominators and set the products equal to each other: (850) x (100) = (80) x (x). Multiplying each side results in the equation 85,000 = 80x.

To solve for *x*, both sides get divided by 80: $\frac{85,000}{80} = \frac{80x}{80}$, resulting in x = 1062.5. Remember that *x* represents the original price. Subtracting the sale price from the original price ($1062.50 – $850) indicates that Frank saved $212.50.

20. C: The decimal points are lined up, with zeroes put in as needed. Then, the numbers are added just like integers:

$$3.40$$

$$2.35$$

$$+4.00$$

$$9.75$$

21. A: This problem can be multiplied as 588×32, except at the end, the decimal point needs to be moved three places to the left. Performing the multiplication will give 18,816, and moving the decimal place over three places results in 18.816.

22. D: The fraction is converted so that the denominator is 100 by multiplying the numerator and denominator by 4, to get $\frac{3}{25} = \frac{12}{100}$. Dividing a number by 100 just moves the decimal point two places to the left, with a result of 0.12.

23. A: Figure out which is largest by looking at the first non-zero digits. Choice *B*'s first non-zero digit is in the hundredths place. The other three all have non-zero digits in the tenths place, so it must be *A*, *C*, or *D*. Of these, *A* has the largest first non-zero digit.

24. C: $40N$ would be 4000% of *N*. It's possible to check that each of the others is actually 40% of *N*.

25. B: Instead of multiplying these out, the product can be estimated by using $18 \times 10 = 180$. The error here should be lower than 15, since it is rounded to the nearest integer, and the numbers add to something less than 30.

26. C: 85% of a number means multiplying that number by 0.85. So, $0.85 \times 20 = \frac{85}{100} \times \frac{20}{1}$, which can be simplified to $\frac{17}{20} \times \frac{20}{1} = 17$.

27. A: To find the fraction of the bill that the first three people pay, the fractions need to be added, which means finding common denominator. The common denominator will be 60. $\frac{1}{5} + \frac{1}{4} + \frac{1}{3} = \frac{12}{60} + \frac{15}{60} + \frac{20}{60} = \frac{47}{60}$. The remainder of the bill is $1 - \frac{47}{60} = \frac{60}{60} - \frac{47}{60} = \frac{13}{60}$.

28. B: 30% is 3/10. The number itself must be 10/3 of 6, or $\frac{10}{3} \times 6 = 10 \times 2 = 20$.

29. A: These numbers to improper fractions: $\frac{11}{3} - \frac{9}{5}$. Take 15 as a common denominator: $\frac{11}{3} - \frac{9}{5} = : \frac{55}{15} - \frac{27}{15} = \frac{28}{15} = 1\frac{13}{15}$ (when rewritten to get rid of the partial fraction).

30. B: Dividing by 98 can be approximated by dividing by 100, which would mean shifting the decimal point of the numerator to the left by 2. The result is 4.2 and rounds to 4.

31. B: $4\frac{1}{3} + 3\frac{3}{4} = 4 + 3 + \frac{1}{3} + \frac{3}{4} = 7 + \frac{1}{3} + \frac{3}{4}$. Adding the fractions gives $\frac{1}{3} + \frac{3}{4} = \frac{4}{12} + \frac{9}{12} = \frac{13}{12} = 1 + \frac{1}{12}$. Thus, $7 + \frac{1}{3} + \frac{3}{4} = 7 + 1 + \frac{1}{12} = 8\frac{1}{12}$.

32. C: The average is calculated by adding all six numbers, then dividing by 6. The first five numbers have a sum of 25. If the total divided by 6 is equal to 6, then the total itself must be 36. The sixth number must be 36 − 25 = 11.

33. B: Multiplying by 10^{-3} means moving the decimal point three places to the left, putting in zeroes as necessary.

34. B: $\frac{5}{2} \div \frac{1}{3} = \frac{5}{2} \times \frac{3}{1} = \frac{15}{2} = 7.5$.

35. A: The total fraction taken up by green and red shirts will be $\frac{1}{3} + \frac{2}{5} = \frac{5}{15} + \frac{6}{15} = \frac{11}{15}$. The remaining fraction is $1 - \frac{11}{15} = \frac{15}{15} - \frac{11}{15} = \frac{4}{15}$.

36. C: If she has used 1/3 of the paint, she has 2/3 remaining. $2\frac{1}{2}$ gallons are the same as $\frac{5}{2}$ gallons. The calculation is $\frac{2}{3} \times \frac{5}{2} = \frac{5}{3} = 1\frac{2}{3}$ gallons.

37. D: The correct answer of 20 °C can be found using the appropriate temperature conversion formula:

$$°C = (°F - 32) \times \frac{5}{9}$$

38. D: The slope is given by the change in *y* divided by the change in *x*. Specifically, it's:

$$slope = \frac{y_2 - y_1}{x_2 - x_1}$$

The first point is (-5,-3) and the second point is (0,-1). Work from left to right when identifying coordinates. Thus the point on the left is point 1 (-5,-3) and the point on the right is point 2 (0,-1).

Now we need to just plug those numbers into the equation:

$$slope = \frac{-1 - (-3)}{0 - (-5)}$$

It can be simplified to:

$$slope = \frac{-1 + 3}{0 + 5}$$

$$slope = \frac{2}{5}$$

39. B: The figure is composed of three sides of a square and a semicircle. The sides of the square are simply added: 9 + 9 + 9 = 27 feet. The circumference of a circle is found by the equation C = 2πr. The radius is 4, so the circumference of the circle is 25.13 ft. Only half of the circle makes up the outer border of the figure (part of the perimeter) so half of 25.13 feet is 12.565 ft. Therefore, the total perimeter is: 27 ft + 12.565 ft = 39.565 ft. The other answer choices use the incorrect formula or fail to include all of the necessary sides.

40. A: The first step is to determine the unknown, which is in terms of the length, l.

The second step is to translate the problem into the equation using the perimeter of a rectangle, $P = 2l + 2w$. The width is the length minus 2 centimeters. The resulting equation is $2l + 2(l - 2) = 44$. The equation can be solved as follows:

$2l + 2l - 4 = 44$	Apply the distributive property on the left side of the equation
$4l - 4 = 44$	Combine like terms on the left side of the equation
$4l = 48$	Add 4 to both sides of the equation
$l = 12$	Divide both sides of the equation by 4

The length of the rectangle is 12 centimeters. The width is the length minus 2 centimeters, which is 10 centimeters. Checking the answers for length and width forms the following equation:

$$44 = 2(12) + 2(10)$$

The equation can be solved using the order of operations to form a true statement: $44 = 44$.

41. B: $3x^2 - 3x + 11$. By distributing the implied one in front of the first set of parentheses and the -1 in front of the second set of parentheses, the parenthesis can be eliminated:

$$1(5x^2 - 3x + 4) - 1(2x^2 - 7) = 5x^2 - 3x + 4 - 2x^2 + 7$$

Next, like terms (same variables with same exponents) are combined by adding the coefficients and keeping the variables and their powers the same: $5x^2 - 3x + 4 - 2x^2 + 7 = 3x^2 - 3x + 11$.

42. D: Three girls for every two boys can be expressed as a ratio: 3:2. This can be visualized as splitting the school into 5 groups: 3 girl groups and 2 boy groups. The number of students that are in each group can be found by dividing the total number of students by 5:

650 divided by 5 equals 1 part, or 130 students per group

To find the total number of girls, the number of students per group (130) is multiplied by the number of girl groups in the school (3). This equals 390, Choice *D*.

43. C: Kimberley worked 4.5 hours at the rate of $10/h and 1 hour at the rate of $12/h. The problem states that her pay is rounded to the nearest hour, so the 4.5 hours would round up to 5 hours at the rate of $10/h. (5h) x ($10/h) + (1h) x ($12/h) = $50 + $12 = $62.

44. B: The first step is to calculate the difference between the larger value and the smaller value.

$$378 - 252 = 126$$

To calculate this difference as a percentage of the original value, and thus calculate the percentage *increase*, 126 is divided by 252, then this result is multiplied by 100 to find the percentage = 50%, answer *B*.

45. A: In order to find the percentage by which the value of the car has been reduced, the current cash value should be divided by the initial value and then multiplied by 100 to find the percentage.

$$\left(\frac{8,000}{20,000}\right) \times 100 = ?$$

$$(.40) \times 100 = 40\%$$

46. A: This problem can be solved by simple multiplication and addition. Since the sale date is over six years apart, 6 can be multiplied by 12 for the number of months in a year, and then the remaining 4 months can be added.

$$(6 \times 12) + 4 = ?$$

$$72 + 4 = 76$$

47. D: This problem can be solved using basic arithmetic. Xavier starts with 20 apples, then gives his sister half, so 20 divided by 2.

$$\frac{20}{2} = 10$$

He then gives his neighbor 6, so 6 is subtracted from 10.

$$10 - 6 = 4$$

Lastly, he uses ¾ of his apples to make an apple pie, so to find remaining apples, the first step is to subtract ¾ from one and then multiply the difference by 4.

$$\left(1 - \frac{3}{4}\right) \times 4 = ?$$

$$\left(\frac{4}{4} - \frac{3}{4}\right) \times 4 = ?$$

$$\left(\frac{1}{4}\right) \times 4 = 1$$

48. C: Nothing is added to x and y since the center is 0 and 5^2 is 25. Choice A is not the correct answer because you do not subtract the radius from x and y. Choice B is not the correct answer because you must square the radius on the right side of the equation. Choice D is not the correct answer because you do not add the radius to x and y in the equation.

49. D: Subtract the center from the x and y values of the equation and square the radius on the right side of the equation. Choice A is not the correct answer because you need to square the radius of the equation. Choice B is not the correct answer because you do not square the centers of the equation. Choice C is not the correct answer because you need to subtract (not add) the centers of the equation.

50. C: Plug in the values for x and y to discover that the solution works, which is $(-3)^2 + (-4)^2 = 25$. Choices A and B are not the correct answers since the solution works. Choice D is not the correct answer because there is enough information to tell where the given point lies on the circle.

51. C: The volume of a cylinder is $\pi r^2 h$, and $\pi \times 6^2 \times 2$ is $72\,\pi$ cm³. Choice A is not the correct answer because that is only $6^2 \times \pi$. Choice B is not the correct answer because that is $2^2 \times 6 \times \pi$. Choice D is not the correct answer because that is $2^3 \times 6 \times \pi$.

52. B: This answer is correct because $3^2 + 4^2$ is $9 + 16$, which is 25. Taking the square root of 25 is 5. Choice A is not the correct answer because that is $3 + 4$. Choice C is not the correct answer because that is stopping at $3^2 + 4^2$ is $9 + 16$, which is 25. Choice D is not the correct answer because that is 3×4.

53.

To solve the problem, a proportion is written consisting of ratios comparing distance and time. One way to set up the proportion is: $\frac{3}{48} = \frac{5}{x}$ $\left(\frac{distance}{time} = \frac{distance}{time}\right)$ where x represents the unknown value of time. To solve a proportion, the ratios are cross-multiplied: $(3)(x) = (5)(48) \rightarrow 3x = 240$. The equation is solved by isolating the variable, or dividing by 3 on both sides, to produce $x = 80$.

54.

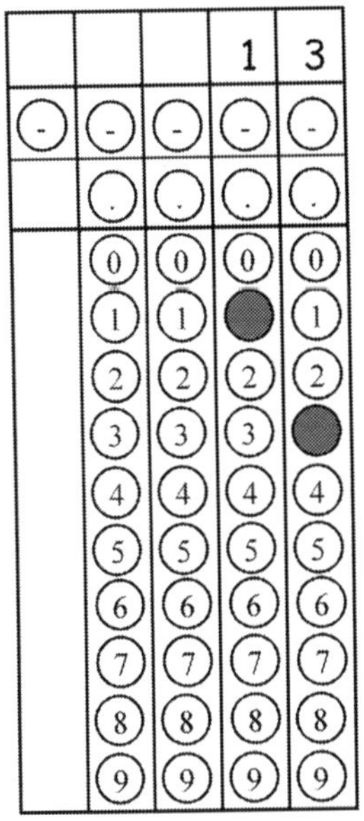

			1	3
⊖	⊖	⊖	⊖	⊖
	⊙	⊙	⊙	⊙
	0	0	0	0
	1	1	●	1
	2	2	2	2
	3	3	3	●
	4	4	4	4
	5	5	5	5
	6	6	6	6
	7	7	7	7
	8	8	8	8
	9	9	9	9

Perimeter is found by calculating the sum of all sides of the polygon. $9 + 9 + 9 + 8 + 8 + s = 56$, where s is the missing side length. Therefore, 43 plus the missing side length is equal to 56. The missing side length is 13 cm.

55.

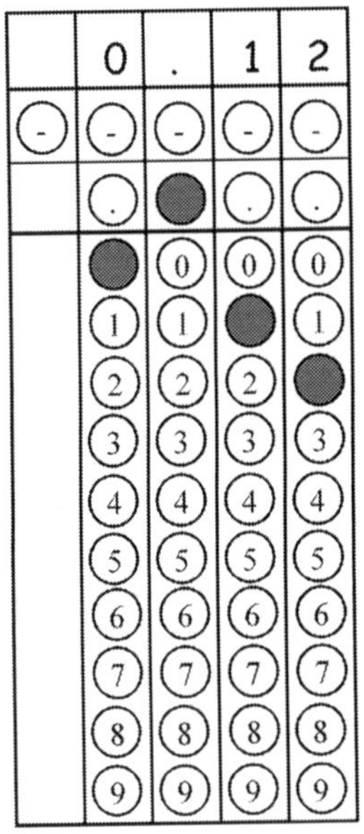

	0	.	1	2
⊖	⊖	⊖	⊖	⊖
	⊙	●	⊙	⊙
●	0		0	0
1	1		●	1
2	2		2	●
3	3		3	3
4	4		4	4
5	5		5	5
6	6		6	6
7	7		7	7
8	8		8	8
9	9		9	9

The fraction is converted so that the denominator is 100 by multiplying the numerator and denominator by 4, to get $\frac{3}{25} = \frac{12}{100}$. Dividing a number by 100 just moves the decimal point two places to the left, with a result of 0.12.

56.

			1	0
⊖	⊖	⊖	⊖	⊖
	○	○	○	○
⓪	⓪	⓪	⓪	●
①	①	①	●	①
②	②	②	②	②
③	③	③	③	③
④	④	④	④	④
⑤	⑤	⑤	⑤	⑤
⑥	⑥	⑥	⑥	⑥
⑦	⑦	⑦	⑦	⑦
⑧	⑧	⑧	⑧	⑧
⑨	⑨	⑨	⑨	⑨

Each instance of x is replaced with a 2, and each instance of y is replaced with a 3 to get $2^2 - 2 \cdot 2 \cdot 3 + 2 \cdot 3^2 = 4 - 12 + 18 = 10$.

57.

			2	
⊖	⊖	⊖	⊖	⊖
	○	○	○	○
⓪	⓪	⓪	⓪	⓪
①	①	①	①	①
②	②	②	●	②
③	③	③	③	③
④	④	④	④	④
⑤	⑤	⑤	⑤	⑤
⑥	⑥	⑥	⑥	⑥
⑦	⑦	⑦	⑦	⑦
⑧	⑧	⑧	⑧	⑧
⑨	⑨	⑨	⑨	⑨

Add 3 to both sides to get $4x = 8$. Then divide both sides by 4 to get $x = 2$.

53.

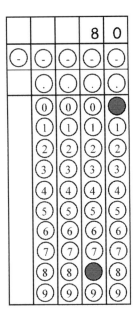

To solve the problem, a proportion is written consisting of ratios comparing distance and time. One way to set up the proportion is: $\frac{3}{48} = \frac{5}{x}$ $\left(\frac{distance}{time} = \frac{distance}{time}\right)$ where x represents the unknown value of time. To solve a proportion, the ratios are cross-multiplied: $(3)(x) = (5)(48) \rightarrow 3x = 240$. The equation is solved by isolating the variable, or dividing by 3 on both sides, to produce $x = 80$.

54.

Perimeter is found by calculating the sum of all sides of the polygon. $9 + 9 + 9 + 8 + 8 + s = 56$, where s is the missing side length. Therefore, 43 plus the missing side length is equal to 56. The missing side length is 13 cm.

55.

	0	.	1	2
⊖	-	-	-	-
	.	●	.	.
	● 0	0	0	0
	1	1	● 1	1
	2	2	2	● 2
	3	3	3	3
	4	4	4	4
	5	5	5	5
	6	6	6	6
	7	7	7	7
	8	8	8	8
	9	9	9	9

The fraction is converted so that the denominator is 100 by multiplying the numerator and denominator by 4, to get $\frac{3}{25} = \frac{12}{100}$. Dividing a number by 100 just moves the decimal point two places to the left, with a result of 0.12.

56.

			1	0
⊖	-	-	-	-
	.	.	.	.
	0	0	0	● 0
	1	1	● 1	1
	2	2	2	2
	3	3	3	3
	4	4	4	4
	5	5	5	5
	6	6	6	6
	7	7	7	7
	8	8	8	8
	9	9	9	9

Each instance of x is replaced with a 2, and each instance of y is replaced with a 3 to get $2^2 - 2 \cdot 2 \cdot 3 + 2 \cdot 3^2 = 4 - 12 + 18 = 10$.

57.

				2
⊖	⊖	⊖	⊖	⊖
	⊙	⊙	⊙	⊙
⓪	⓪	⓪	⓪	⓪
①	①	①	①	①
②	②	②	②	●
③	③	③	③	③
④	④	④	④	④
⑤	⑤	⑤	⑤	⑤
⑥	⑥	⑥	⑥	⑥
⑦	⑦	⑦	⑦	⑦
⑧	⑧	⑧	⑧	⑧
⑨	⑨	⑨	⑨	⑨

Add 3 to both sides to get $4x = 8$. Then divide both sides by 4 to get $x = 2$..

Dear SHSAT Test Taker,

We would like to start by thanking you for purchasing this study guide for your SHSAT exam. We hope that we exceeded your expectations.

Our goal in creating this study guide was to cover all of the topics that you will see on the test. We also strove to make our practice questions as similar as possible to what you will encounter on test day. With that being said, if you found something that you feel was not up to your standards, please send us an email and let us know.

We would also like to let you know about other books in our catalog that may interest you.

SHSAT Practice Tests:

This can be found on Amazon: amazon.com/dp/1628455284

SAT

amazon.com/dp/1628454679

ACT

amazon.com/dp/1628454709

ACCUPLACER

amazon.com/dp/162845492X

AP Biology

amazon.com/dp/1628454989

SAT Math 1

amazon.com/dp/1628454717

We have study guides in a wide variety of fields. If the one you are looking for isn't listed above, then try searching for it on Amazon or send us an email.

Thanks Again and Happy Testing!
Product Development Team
info@studyguideteam.com

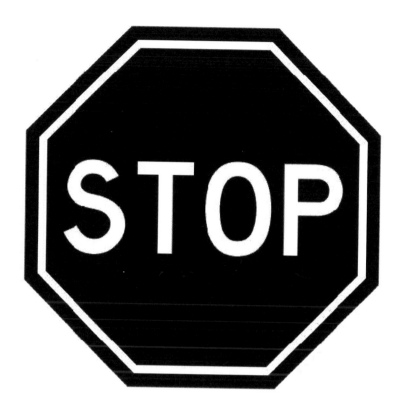

FREE Test Taking Tips DVD Offer

To help us better serve you, we have developed a Test Taking Tips DVD that we would like to give you for FREE. **This DVD covers world-class test taking tips that you can use to be even more successful when you are taking your test.**

All that we ask is that you email us your feedback about your study guide. Please let us know what you thought about it – whether that is good, bad or indifferent.

To get your **FREE Test Taking Tips DVD**, email freedvd@studyguideteam.com with "FREE DVD" in the subject line and the following information in the body of the email:

    a. The title of your study guide.

    b. Your product rating on a scale of 1-5, with 5 being the highest rating.

    c. Your feedback about the study guide. What did you think of it?

    d. Your full name and shipping address to send your free DVD.

If you have any questions or concerns, please don't hesitate to contact us at freedvd@studyguideteam.com.

Thanks again!

Made in the USA
Middletown, DE
25 May 2018